TOWARDS UNDERSTANDING ISLAM

QUR'AN FOUNDATION
NON PROFIT

An Islamic Educational Org.
(503) 776-5968
1257 Siskiyou Blvd. #224
Ashland, OR 97520 USA

TOWARDS UNDERSTANDING
ISLAM

By
A.A. MAUDUDI

CONTENTS

(iv)

FOREWORD

This is not only a new translation of TOWARDS UN-DERSTANDING ISLAM, but is also an entirely new and revised edition of it.

The purpose of this book is to provide all those persons —Muslims and non-Muslims—who have no access to the original sources of Islam, with a brief but clear and comprehensive view of Islam. This is why a discussion of minute details has been avoided and why we have sought to portray the entire picture of Islam in one perspective. We have not confined the book to stating what Muslims believe in and stand for, but have also tried to explain the rational bases of these beliefs. Similarly, we have not only presented the Islamic methods of worship and the outlines of the Islamic way of life but have also tried to unveil the wisdom behind them. We hope this book will go a long way toward satisfying the intellectual cravings of the Muslim youth and will help non-Muslims in understanding Islam.

A. A. Maududi

CHAPTER ONE

THE MEANING OF ISLAM

Nearly every religion of the world has been named after either the person it has been associated with or after the people or nation from which it originated. For example, Christianity derives its name from Jesus Christ; Buddhism from Gautama Buddha; Zoroastrianism from Zoroaster; and Judaism, the religion of the Jews, takes its name from both the tribe of Judah and the country of Judea where it was born. The same is true of other religions. But not so with Islam. This religion enjoys the unique distinction of having no such association with any particular person or people. The word 'Islam' does not convey any such relationship—for it does not belong to any certain person, people, or country. Nor is it the product of any human mind. It is a universal religion and its objective is to create and cultivate within man the quality and attitude of Islam.

'Islam', in fact, is a descriptive title. Whoever possesses the qualities contained within this title, regardless of his race, community, country, or family, is a Muslim. According to the Qur'an (the holy book of the Muslims), among every society and in all ages there have been good and righteous people who possessed these qualities—and all of them were and are Muslims.

This automatically brings us to the question: What does Islam mean? And who is a Muslim?

ISLAM—What does it mean?

'Islam' is an Arabic word meaning submission, surrender, and obedience. As a religion, Islam[1] stands for complete submission and obedience to God—and this is why it

---

[1] Islam also stands for and means peace as it is derived from the word **Salam.**

1

is called 'ISLAM'.

Everyone can see that we live in an orderly universe. There is law and order among all the parts that make up this universe. Everything is assigned a place in a grand scheme which is working in a magnificent and superb way. The sun, the moon, the stars, in fact all the heavenly bodies are knit together in a splendid system. These bodies follow an unalterable law and do not make even the slightest deviation from their ordained course. The earth rotates on its axis and in its revolution around the sun follows the path laid out for it with precision. In fact, everything in the world, from the tiny whirling electron to the mighty galaxy, constantly and ceaselessly follows its own laws. Matter, energy, and life—all obey laws, laws by which they must grow or change, live or die. Even in the human world, the laws of nature are quite obvious. Man's birth, growth, and life are all regulated by a set of biological laws. He derives nourishment from nature according to a law which cannot be changed. In fact, all the organs of his body from the small tissues to the heart and brain are operating according to the laws set out for them. In short, ours is a law-governed universe and everything in it is following the course that has been ordained for it.

This all-powerful and all-penetrating law, which governs everything that exists, from the tiniest particles of matter to the magnificent galaxies in the high heavens is the law of God, the Creator and Ruler of the universe. Since all created things obey the law of God, the entire universe, therefore, literally follows the system of Islam—for Islam signifies nothing but obedience and submission to God, the Lord of the universe. The sun, the moon, the earth and all other heavenly bodies are thus 'Muslims' (obedient servants of God). So are the air, water, and soil and all living things like the insects, birds, and mammals of the animal world, as well as the shrubs, trees, vegetables and fruits of the plant world. Everything in the universe is 'Muslim'; for they all obey God Almighty by submitting to His laws. Even the man who denies the existence of God, or decides to worship someone other than God, is obligated to be a 'Muslim' as far as his bodily existence is concerned. For this man's entire life, from the embryonic stage to the dissolution of the body into dust after death, must follow the course prescribed for it by God's law. His every molecule, every tissue and limb of his body must endlessly obey the universal laws laid down for them by Almighty God. His tongue, which because of his ignorance advocates the denial of God or states that several gods exist, is by its very nature a 'Muslim'. His head, which he willingly bows to others besides God, is a *born Muslim*. His heart wherein, through his lack of true knowledge, he cherishes love and reverence for others is 'Muslim' by intuition. These are all obedient to the Divine Law, and their functions and operations are governed by the Commandments of that law alone.

This is, in short, the real position of man and the universe. Let's now examine this problem from a different point of view. Man's character is such that there are two separate aspects of his life, two distinct spheres of his activity. In one sphere he finds himself totally regulated by the Divine Law. He cannot budge an inch or move a step away from it. Nor can he in any way slip away from its all-embracing control. For example, man has no control over the power of nature; natural disasters occur and he can neither evade them nor limit their course. In one area of the earth, hurricanes and tropical storms predominate, in another severely cold weather and snow storms, in yet another devastating tornadoes, earthquakes and volcanoes. Man can find no refuge on the globe from such events, and when they occur in full force, he often calls upon that very God Who controls these processes, Whose help he didn't bother to seek until disaster struck.[2]

But there is another sphere of his activity as well. He has been blessed with reason and intelligence. He has the power to think and make judgments, to select or reject, to adopt or spurn. He is free to adopt whatever way of life he chooses. He can select any religion, assume any way of life, and fashion his living according to whatever ideologies he likes. He may prepare his own code of conduct or accept

---

[2] The Editors.

one made by someone else. He has been bestowed with *free will* and can chalk out his course of behavior. In this respect, he, unlike any other creature, has been given freedom of choice, thought, and action.

Both of these aspects are realistic, coexisting yet individually distinguishable parts of man's life.

In the first, like all other creatures, man is a born Muslim, constantly obeys the orders of Almighty God, and is bound to remain doing so. As far as the second aspect is concerned, he is free to become or not to become a Muslim. Here is where his gift of freedom of choice is operable— and it is the way a person exercises this freedom which divides mankind into two groups: believers and non-believers. An individual who chooses to recognize his Creator, accepts Him as his real Master, honestly and faithfully submits to His laws and orders, and follows the system of life He has revealed for man, thereby becomes a perfect Muslim. Such a man has achieved completeness in his Islam by consciously deciding to obey God through the use of those very abilities of free thought, choice and action which God Almighty blessed him with. Now his entire life has become one of obedience to God. There is now no conflict in his personality because he spends his time and energy working for the pleasure of his Creator. He is a perfect Muslim and his Islam is complete—as this submission of his entire self to the will of God is Islam and nothing but Islam.

He has now consciously submitted to Him Whom he had already been obeying unconsciously. He has now willingly offered obedience to the Master Whom he already owed obedience unintentionally. His knowledge is now real for he has acknowledged the Being Who blessed him with the power to learn and know. Now his reasoning and judgment are set on an even plane—for he has correctly decided to obey the Being Who in fact gave him those abilities of thinking and judging. His tongue is now in its natural state for it truthfully asserts that it is the Lord Most High Who gave it the faculty of speech. In fact, his entire living is an example of truth for, in all areas of life, he voluntarily as well as involuntarily obeys the laws of the same One God —the Master of the universe. And by so doing he worships Him whom the whole universe worships. This is the natural condition. And such a man is truly God's representative on earth. The whole world is for him and he is for God.

THE NATURE OF DISBELIEF (KUFR)

In contrast to the man described above is the example of a man who, although born a Muslim, does not use his skills of reason, intelligence and intuition for recognizing his Lord and Creator. Rather, he misuses his freedom of choice by *choosing* to deny Him. Such a man becomes a *disbeliever* due to his rejection of God.

The Arabic word for disbelief is *kufr*, which literally means "to cover" or "to conceal". The man who rejects God is called a concealer (kafir) because he conceals *by his disbelief* what is inherently in his nature and what is embalmed within his soul. For, indeed his nature is instinctively imbued with 'Islam'. His whole body, every cell and each atom, functions in obedience to that instinct. Each and every particle that exists—living or lifeless— functions in accordance with 'Islam' and is fulfilling the duty that has been assigned to it. But the vision of this man has been blurred, his common sense has been befogged, and he is unable to see the obvious. His own nature has become hidden from his eyes and he thinks and acts totally disregarding it. The real truth becomes separated from him and he gropes in the dark—such is the nature of *disbelief.*

Disbelief (kufr) is not a form of ignorance, rather it *is* ignorance, pure and simple. What ignorance could be greater than to be ignorant of God, the Creator, the Lord of the universe? A person observes the vast panorama of nature, the superb mechanism that is ceaselessly working, the grand design that exists in every nook and corner of the creation—he observes this endless machinery, but does not know who is its Maker and Director. He looks at his own body, the wonderful organism that operates in an intelligible and systematic fashion, and uses it to achieve

5

whatever goals he wishes. Yet he is unable to comprehend the Force that brought it into existence, the Engineer Who designed and produced this machine, the Creator Who made this unique living being out of lifeless matter: carbon, calcium, sodium and the like. He sees how impressive is the plan by which the universe operates—but fails to see the Planner behind it. He sees great beauty and harmony in its workings — but not the Creator Who allows it to work. He observes the wonderful design of nature — but not the Designer!

No matter which way he turns in the world about him, he sees magnificent examples of skill in science and wisdom, mathematics and engineering, design and purpose. Yet he blinds himself to the Being Who brought into existence all that is in this endless universe. How can a man who has blinded himself to this great and important reality approach the true perspectives of knowledge? How can the prospects of truth and knowledge be opened to such a man? How can anyone who has started out in the wrong place reach the right destination? He will fail to find the clue to Reality. The Right Path will remain hidden from him, and whatever his efforts in science and the arts, he will never be able to discover the lights of truth and wisdom. He will be groping in darkness and stumbling in the gloom of ignorance.

But this is not all; *disbelief* is also a form of tyranny, in fact, the worst of tyrannies. And what is 'tyranny'? It is an act of cruel and unjust use of any force or power. If you force a thing to act unjustly or to act against its true nature, its will and natural inclination, that is tyranny, root and branch.

We have seen that whatever is in the universe is obedient to God Almighty, the Creator of all that the world contains. To obey, to live according to His Will and Law, or to put it more precisely, *to be a Muslim* is ingrained in the nature of things. God has given man power over these things, but it is superimposed upon their nature that they should be used to fulfill the Will and Law of God and not otherwise. But the person who disobeys God and resorts to *disbelief* perpetrates the greatest of injustices, for he uses all these God-given powers of body and mind to rebel against his natural state and becomes an unwilling instrument in the drama of disobedience. He forces his head to bow before gods other than the One True God. He cherishes in his heart the love, reverence and fear of other powers, totally disregarding the instinctive urge of his mind. He uses his power and the powers of all those things upon which he has authority against the natural inclination of things, against the expressed will of God. By this he establishes a reign of tyranny. Can there be a greater example of injustice, tyranny, and cruelty than that exhibited by this man who exploits and misuses everything under the sun and forces them to follow a course that is against nature and justice?

Disbelief is not mere tyranny; it is, at the very least, sheer rebellion, ingratitude and treachery. After all, what is man's real nature? What kind of power and authority does he have? Is he himself the creator of his mind, his heart, his soul, and other parts of his body—or have they been created by God? Was it he who created the universe and all that is within her—or has it been created by God? Who has harnessed countless powers and energies for the service of man, oil and electricity, sunlight and atomic forces—man or God? If everything has been constructed by God and God alone, then to whom do they belong? Who is their real owner? Who is their rightful guardian? Clearly, it is God and none else. And if God is the Creator, the Master, and the Sovereign, then who could be a greater rebel than the man who uses God's creation against his own regulations—who forces his mind to plot against God, harbors in his soul thoughts against Him, and uses his various abilities against the Almighty's will. If a servant betrays his master, you denounce him as faithless. If an army officer becomes disloyal to the state, you proclaim him a traitor and renegade. If a person cheats on his friend, you don't hesitate to condemn him as an ingrate. But what match can this betrayal, this ingratitude, and this rebellion have to the one which the disbeliever commits by his denial of God? After all, who is the source of all power and authority? Who gave man command over the resources? Who elevated people to positions of authority and power? Who gave presidents, kings, and governors the power to rule and Who is the true provider and distributor of wealth? All such things which men possess and anything good which man uses to help others, are gifts from God. The greatest obligation a man has is to his parents. But who has implanted the parents' hearts with the desire to love and cherish their children? Who gave the mother the will and power to nurture and nourish her children?

A little reflection will reveal that God is the greatest caretaker of man. He is the Creator, Master, Nourisher, Sustainer, as well as the real King and President. And this being the position of God as contrasted to man, what greater betrayal, ingratitude, rebellion, and treason can there be than *kufr (disbelief)*, through which a man denies and disobeys his real Master and Ruler?

Do you think that man, by living the life of disobedience and denial, can do any harm to God Almighty? No, not in the least. Man is an insignificant speck on the face of a tiny sphere within this limitless universe. What harm can he do to the Master of the universe whose territories are so infinitely huge that we cannot even come close to exploring their boundaries with the help of the most powerful telescope or fastest spacecraft? What harm can he do to a God Whose power is so great that uncountable heavenly bodies like the earth, moon, sun, and stars are at His command, whirling like tiny balls; Whose wealth is so boundless that He is the sole Master and Controller of the whole universe; Who provides for all and needs none to provide for Him? Man's revolt against Him can do Him no harm. On the contrary, by his disobedience, man walks the path that will lead him to total ruin and disgrace.

The inevitable result of this revolt against and denial of reality is a failure to achieve the basic and farthest-reaching purposes and concepts for life. These great concepts of truth were created for man by God Himself. However, this rebel will not find the thread of true knowledge and vision. He will never find this knowledge for he has denied the existence of the One Who created it. His intelligence and reason will always run astray. For reasoning which fails to recognize the Being Who created it cannot brighten the walkways of life. And without this clear light brightening his way, man can never recognize and put these truths into practice in his daily life.

The result is that a man like this will meet with failure in all affairs of his life. His moral, civil, and social life, his struggle for prosperity and his family life, in short, his whole life will be in turmoil. Disorder and confusion will be spread on the earth by him. He will, without the least reservation, shed blood, violate the rights of others, be cruel to them and tyrannize them. By this behavior, he will create a general atmosphere of disorder and destruction in the world. His perverted mind, blurred vision, distorted values, and evil-generating activities would make life miserable for both himself and those associated with him. Such a man will destroy the peace and calm of life on earth: tyranny and arrogance, destruction and decimation will be the result. And in the life hereafter, he would be held guilty for the crimes he committed against his nature, skills, and resources. Every organ of his body—his brain, eyes, hands, and feet—will complain against the injustice and cruelty he did to them. Every tissue of his body will belittle him before God Who, as the fountain of all justice, will award him the full punishment he deserves. This is the inglorious consequence of *disbelief*. It leads to the blind alley of total failure, here and in the hereafter.

THE BLESSINGS OF ISLAM

After surveying the evils and disadvantages of disbelief, let's now examine the blessings of Islam.

In the world around you, as well as in your immediate environment, you find countless indications of God's divine power. This majestic universe which ceaselessly operates with unmatched order and organization, which functions in harmony with laws that cannot be changed, is in itself witness that its Creator, Designer, and Governor is a Great Being Who has knowledge and power over all things. It is witness that this Being has command over limitless resources, a Being Whose wisdom is perfect, and Whom nothing in this universe dare disobey. It is within the nature of man and everything else in this universe to obey Him. In fact, man is constantly obeying His Law even though he may be unaware of it; and the moment he disrupts this Law, he is exposed to death and destruction. This is the law of nature, our everyday observance.

Besides giving man the capability to gain knowledge, the ability to think and ponder, and the sense for distinguishing right from wrong, God granted him a certain amount of freedom of will and action. It is within this freedom that man's real test in this world lies. His knowledge and intelligence, his ability to tell the good from the bad, and his freedom of will and action are constantly being tried and tested. In this trial, man has not been forced to follow a specific direction, for the objective of the trial would be defeated by compulsion. If, while taking an exam, you are forced to write down a certain answer to a question, the examination will be of no use. Your proficiency can be properly judged only if you are allowed to answer the question freely and according to what you know about the subject at hand. If your answer is wrong, you will fail and your failure will hinder your future success and progress. The situation faced by man in this world is precisely the same. God has given man freedom of will and action so that he can be free to select whatever way of life he likes and considers proper for himself—Islam or *disbelief.*

On one hand, there is the type of man who understands neither the nature of himself nor that of the universe. He errs in recognizing who his real Master is, fails to visualize His qualities, and misuses his freedom by pursuing the path of disobedience and revolt. Such a man has failed in the trial of how his knowledge, intelligence, and responsibility were supposed to be used. He has failed to rise to the standard for which he was made, and does not deserve a better destiny than the one discussed above.

On the other hand, there is another man who emerges successful in this trial. By correctly using his knowledge and intelligence, he recognizes his Creator, firmly believes in Him, and, in spite of being under no compulsion to do so, chooses the path of obedience to Him. He does not err in telling the right from the wrong, and chooses to follow what is correct despite having the potential to lean towards evil. He understands his nature, realizes the laws and truths of that nature, and despite being free and able to select any direction, adopts the way of obedience and loyalty to God the Creator. He is successful in this trial because he has properly used his ability to think and reason. His other skills bear witness to this truth as well. He uses his eyes to see the reality, his ears to listen to the Truth, his mind to form correct opinions, and puts his whole heart and soul into following the correct way he has chosen. He chooses Truth, sees the Reality, and willingly and joyfully submits to his Lord and Master. He is intelligent, truthful, and dutiful, for he has chosen light over darkness, and, after seeing this light, has responded to it with great enthusiasm. Thus, he has proved by his conduct that he is not only a seeker after Truth, but recognizes it and worships it as well. Clearly, he is on the Right Path and is bound to succeed in this world and in the life to come.

Such a man will always select the Right Plan in every field of knowledge and activity. The man who knows God by recognizing all His attributes knows the beginning of as well as the ultimate end of Reality. He can never be led astray, for his first step is on the right path, and he is sure of the direction and destination towards which his life is moving. In philosophy, he will ponder over the secrets of the universe, and will try to understand the mysteries of nature, but, unlike an unbelieving philosopher, he will not lose his way in the maze of doubt and skepticism. His path being illuminated with Divine Vision, every step he takes will fall in the right direction. In science, he will try to understand the laws of nature, uncover the hidden treasures of the earth, and direct all the hitherto unknown forces of mind and matter—all for the betterment of mankind. He will try his level best to explore all avenues of knowledge and research and will try to harness all that exists in the earth and heavens in the interest of mankind. At every stage of his inquiry, his God-consciousness will save him from using science and the scientific methods for evil and destructive purposes. He will never imagine himself nor claim to be the master of all that is in the universe, boasting to be a conqueror of nature, arrogating to himself godly and sovereign powers, and maintaining the ambition of subverting the world. He will not seek to subdue the human race or oppress the people. Nor will he attempt to establish his supremacy over everyone and everything by any means fair or foul. Such an attitude of revolt and defiance can never be entertained by a Muslim scientist— only an *unbelieving* scientist can become a victim of such illusions and by serving them expose the entire human race to the danger of total destruction and annihilation!

In contrast, a Muslim scientist will behave in a totally different way. The deeper his insight into science, the stronger will be his faith in God. His head will bow down before Him in gratitude. He will feel that since his Master has blessed him with greater power and knowledge, he must work hard for his own good as well as the good of humanity. His freedom will not be used to promote violence and destruction. He will be guided by the tenets of morality and Divine Revelation. Thus, instead of becoming an instrument of destruction, science would become an agency for the welfare of humanity. In this manner, he will express his gratefulness to his Master for the gifts and blessings he has given man.

In the same way, in history, economics, politics, law, and other branches of arts and science, a Muslim will nowhere lag behind an *unbeliever*. Yet the way they view these fields and the procedures they use to gain knowledge in them will differ widely. A Muslim will study every branch of knowledge, but will keep that knowledge in its proper perspective. He will work hard in pursuing the proper objective of life and, through his study, will arrive at proper conclusions. In history, he will learn from the past experiences of mankind and will discover the true causes for the rise and fall of civilizations. He will try to benefit from all that was good and correct in the past and will be careful to avoid anything which led to the decline and fall of nations. In politics his sole objective will be to strive for the establishment of a government wherein peace, brotherhood, and goodness reign. He will seek to build that government wherein every human being is a brother to one another, where no form of exploitation or slavery is rampant, and where the rights of the individual are respectfully upheld. He will seek to build that government wherein the powers of the state are considered a sacred trust from God and are used for the common welfare of all. In the field of law, the Muslim will seek to make it a true example of justice and an authentic protector of the rights of all—particularly of the weak. He will make sure that all get their due share and no injustice or oppression is inflicted on anyone. He will respect the law, make others respect it, and will see that it is administered justly and fairly.

The moral life of a Muslim will always be filled with godliness, righteousness, and truthfulness. He will live in the world with the belief that God alone is the Master of all, that whatever he and other men possess is a gift from God, that the powers he wields are only a trust from God. He will think that the freedom he has been endowed with is not to be used indiscriminately, and that it is in his interest to use it in agreement with God's Will. He will constantly keep in mind that one day he will have to return to God Almighty and submit an account of his entire life. Such a sense of accountability will remain so firmly implanted in his mind that he will never behave in a carefree or irresponsible manner.

Think of the moral excellence of the man who lives with this frame of thought: his will be a life of purity, piety, love, and altruism. He will be a blessing unto mankind. His thinking will not be polluted with wicked thoughts and perverted ambitions. He will abstain from seeing evil, hearing evil, and doing evil. He will guard his tongue and never utter even a single lie. He will earn his living through just and fair means, and would rather go hungry than eat food which was acquired through exploitation and injustice. He will neither oppress the people nor violate human life and honor regardless of its form or color. He will never yield to the forces of evil and corruption, regardless of what such opposition may cost him. He will be an example of goodness and excellence and will uphold truth and justice even at the cost of his own life. He will abhor all forms of injustice and will stand firm for truth, undaunted by the storms of adversity. Such a man will be a power to be reckoned with. He is bound to succeed. Nothing on earth can discourage him or impede his way.

He will be the most honored and respected one. No one can surpass him in this respect. How can humiliation ever overcome a person who is not prepared to bow his head or even spread his hand for any favor before anyone except God Almighty, the Master of the universe?

He will be the most powerful, the most effective. No one can be more powerful than he—for he fears none but God and seeks blessings from no one but Him. What power can make him deviate from the right path? What force can mold his conscience? What could possibly coerce his behavior?

He will be the most wealthy and rich. No one in the world can be richer or more independent than he—for he will live a life of simplicity, satisfaction, and contentment. He will neither be impure, indulgent, nor greedy. He will be satisfied with whatever he earns fairly and honestly; even if heaps of ill-received wealth are put before him, he would not like to look at them, let alone try to benefit from them. His heart will be full of peace and contentment— and what wealth can be greater than this?

He will be most respected, popular, and loved. No one can be more lovable than he—for he lives a life of charity and kindness. He will do justice to everyone and everything he meets, discharge his duties honestly, and work for the good of others with sincerity. People's hearts will naturally be drawn to him and they will love and respect him.

14

He will be most trusted and honored. No one can be more truthworthy than he—for he will not betray his trust, nor will he go astray from righteousness. He will be true to his world and honest in his transactions. Fairness and justice will be the rule in all his affairs, for he is certain that God is present everywhere and is always aware and watching. Words fail to describe the credit and goodwill that such a man commands. Can there be anyone who will not trust him? Such is the life and character of a Muslim.

If you understand the character of a true Muslim, you will be convinced he can not live in humiliation, debasement, or subjugation. He is bound to prevail. No power on earth can overwhelm or subdue him. Islam instills in him the qualities which cannot be overshadowed by any attraction, pleasure, or illusion.

And after living a respectable and honorable life on earth, he will return to his Creator Who will shower upon him the choicest of His blessings. God will bestow these blessings on him because he discharged his duty ably, fulfilled his mission successfully, and emerged from the trial triumphantly. He is successful in life in this world and in the hereafter and will live in eternal peace, joy, and happiness.

This is Islam, the natural religion of man, the religion which is not associated with any person, people, period, or place. In every age, in every country, and among every people, all God-knowing and truth-loving men have believed and lived this very religion. They were all Muslims, whether they called their way Islam or something else. Whatever its name was, it signified Islam and nothing but Islam.

CHAPTER TWO

FAITH AND OBEDIENCE

Islam means obedience to God. Common sense tells us that this obedience cannot be fully practiced unless man knows certain basic facts of life and places firm faith in them. What are those facts? What are the essentials which a man must know about so he can fashion his life according to the Divine System? This we propose to discuss in the present chapter.

First of all, one should have unshakable belief in the existence of God, for unless a man firmly believes in God's existence, how can he be obedient to Him?

One must also know the attributes of God. It is the knowledge of the attributes of God which enables man to cultivate within the noblest of human qualities and to fashion his life in virtue and godliness. If a man does not know that there is One and only One God Who is the Creator, Ruler, and Sustainer of the universe and there is none else to share with Him even a shred of the divine power and authority, he may fall prey to false gods. He may even offer his homage to them to solicit their favor. But if he knows the divine attribute of the Oneness of God, there is not the least possibility of his falling prey to this illusion. If a man knows that God sees, hears, and knows everything we do in public or in private—even our thoughts—then how can he afford to be defiant and disobedient to God? He will feel he is under eternal watch, and will therefore behave in the most appropriate way. But he who is not aware of these attributes may be misled, because of his ignorance, into disobedience of God. The qualities and attributes which a man must possess if he wants to pursue the way of Islam, can be developed only by having a complete knowledge of the attributes of God.

It is the knowledge of God's attributes and characteristics which purifies a man's mind and soul, his beliefs, morals, and actions. A mere cursory acquaintance or an academic knowledge of these attributes is not sufficient for the task ahead. Rather, a man must have a strong conviction rooted deep in his mind so that he can remain free from insidious doubts and perversions.

Also, man must know in detail the *way of living* which he needs to follow in order to seek the pleasure of God. Unless a man knows the likes and dislikes of God, how can he choose and adopt the godly path and reject the other? If a man has no knowledge of the Divine Law, how can he follow it? In this respect, knowledge of the Divine Law, that is, realizing that the Divinely Revealed System of Life exists is extremely important.

But here again, mere knowledge will not be sufficient. Man must have full confidence, he must be totally convinced that it is the *Divine Law* and that his *salvation lies in following this Law alone.* For knowledge without this firm belief will fail to stimulate man toward the Right Path, and he may be lost in the blind alley of disobedience.

Finally, man must know what the consequences of belief and obedience are as contrasted to those of disbelief and disobedience. He must know what blessings would be showered upon him if he chooses God's way and leads a life of purity, virtue, and obedience. He must also realize what wicked and painful consequences would result if he adopts the way of disobedience and revolt. For this purpose, knowledge of life after death is absolutely essential. Man must have an unshakable belief that death does not mean the end of life. He must know without question that there will be resurrection and he will be brought to the highest court of justice, to be presided over by God Almighty Himself. He must know that on that Day of Judgment complete justice will prevail, and that good deeds will be rewarded and misdeeds punished. Everybody will get his due and there is no escape. This is bound to happen.

This sense of responsibility and accountability is essential for full-fledged obedience to the Law of God.

A man who has no knowledge of the world to come may consider obedience or disobedience to be immaterial. He may think that the obedient and disobedient will both meet a similar end; he thinks that after death, both will be reduced to dust. With this attitude, how can he be expected to submit to all the inconveniences and hardships associated with the life of active obedience? How could he be expected to shun sins which don't seem to bring him any moral or material loss in this world? By thinking this way, a man cannot submit to God's Law. Nor can a man who lacks firm belief in a life after death and in the Divine Court of Judgment, remain strong and steadfast in the turbulent water of life with its sin, crime, and evil. Doubt and hesitancy rob a man of his will to action. You can remain firm in your behavior only if you are firm in your beliefs. If your mind wavers, you cannot remain solid in your convictions. You can whole-heartedly follow a course only if you are sure of the benefits you will gain by following it and of the losses and grievances that will engulf you if you disobey it. Thus, to channel one's life into obedience to God, a profound knowledge of the consequences of belief and disbelief and of the life after death is required.

These facts are essential and the understanding of them must be clear if one wants to live the life of obedience, i.e. Islam.

Faith: What does it mean?

We described the concept of faith in the previous discussion as 'knowledge and belief'. The Arabic word *iman* which we have translated into English as *faith* literally means 'to know', 'to believe' and 'to be convinced beyond a shadow of a doubt'. Thus, faith is firm belief arising out of knowledge and conviction. The man who knows of and puts full trust in belief in the Oneness of God, His qualities, His Revealed guidance, and in the Divine mechanism of reward and punishment is called *mu'min* or *faithful*. Such faith must direct man into a life of active obedience to the Will of Almighty God. And the person who lives this life of obedience is known as a Muslim.

This should clearly bring home the fact that without faith no man can be a true Muslim. It is the indispensible essential; rather, it is the starting point without which no beginning can be made. The relation of Islam to faith is the same as a tree to its seed. As a tree cannot sprout forth without its seed, in the same way it is not possible for a man, who doesn't have any belief to begin with, to become a 'Muslim'. On the other hand, just as a tree may not grow from a planted seed, and even if it sprouts, its growth may be impaired or retarded, in the same way, a man may have faith, but due to a number of weaknesses, may not become a true and staunch Muslim. Thus we find that faith is the starting point. We find that it leads man to the life of submission to God, and that there is no way a man can become a Muslim without faith. On the contrary, it is possible that a man may have faith but, because of the weakness of his will power, poor upbringing or bad company, may not be living the life of a true Muslim. The above description allows us to classify all men into four categories according to the concept of Islamic *faith*:

1. Those who have firm faith—a faith that makes them completely and whole-heartedly submit to God. They follow the system of God and devote themselves completely to seeking his pleasure. They do everything He likes and avoid all that He dislikes. In fact, their love of God is greater than their love for themselves. In their extreme devotion, they are even more fervent than is the typical man in pursuit of wealth and power. Such men are true Muslims.

2. Those who have faith, who believe in God, His Rules and the Day of Judgment, but whose faith is not deep and strong enough to make them totally submit to Him. They are far below the rank of true Muslims and deserve punishment for the wrongs they commit, but Muslims they remain.

3. Those who do not possess faith at all. These people refuse to acknowledge the sovereignty of God and are rebels. Even if their behavior is not bad and even if they are not spreading corruption and violence, they remain

rebels and their apparent good deeds are of little value. Such men are like outlaws. And just as when a certain action of an outlaw is in harmony with the law of the land, he still doesn't become a loyal citizen, neither does the apparent good of those who revolt against God compensate for the degree of wrong, rebellion, and disobedience they perpetrate by denying their real Master.

4. Those who neither possess faith nor do good deeds. They spread disorder in the world, corruption on earth, and perpetrate all kinds of violence and oppression. They are the worst of all people; for they are rebels as well as wrong-doers and criminals.

The above classification clearly shows that man's real success and salvation depend on *faith*. The life of obedience (Islam) is born from the seed of this faith. This Islam of a person may be flawless or defective. But without faith there can be no Islam. Where there is no Islam there is *Kufr* (total disbelief). Its form and nature may differ in any given case, but in every way it is *Kufr* and nothing but *Kufr*.

How to acquire the knowledge of God

Now the question arises: How does one acquire the knowledge of and belief in God, His attributes, His Law, and the Day of Judgment?

We already referred to the countless manifestations of God all around us. All this bears witness that there is One and only One Creator and Governor of this universe and that it is He Who controls and directs it. These evidences reflect the divine titles of the Creator: His great wisdom, His endless knowledge, His mercy, His limitless Power. In short, His attributes can be traced everywhere in His works. But man's intellect and his ability to attain knowledge has made a big mistake in observing and understanding these obvious qualities. These are all so clear and our eyes are open to read what is written large on the creation. But here men have made serious errors. Some declared that there are two gods, and others began to profess belief in trinity. Some began nature worship and others divided godhood into various deities; gods of rain, air, fire, life, death, etc. Even though the evidences of God's Oneness were quite clear, human reason failed to see the reality in its true perspective. It faltered and stumbled, meeting deception after deception and resulted in nothing but a confused state of mind. To expand further on the errors of human judgment would require a whole different discussion in itself and it is not our purpose to do so here.

With regard to life after death, men have also forwarded many erroneous notions. For instance, some claimed that man is reduced to dust after death and will not rise to life again. Others say that man is subject to a process of continuous regeneration (reincarnation) and is punished or rewarded in this world or in oncoming cycles of worldly life.

Even greater problems arise when we approach the question of the system of life man should follow. For a man to devise a complete and balanced format for living that would conform to God's pleasure is an extremely difficult task. Even the man who is equipped with the highest talents of reason and intelligence, who possesses matchless wisdom, and who has the experience of many years of deep thought and deliberation, even then the chances of his constructing the correct views of life are not very promising. If, after life-long deliberation, he succeeds in this achievement, he will lack the confidence that he really discovered the Truth and selected the correct road.

Although the most difficult test of man's wisdom may have been to leave him to his resources without any external guidance so he could find the correct way for living in this world, those who were more capable to sort, sift, and strive might have reached the truth and would have won success and salvation, while those not reaching it would have failed. But the All-Knowing God spared His human creatures such a hard task. Because of His infinite Mercy, God sent special men to mankind. He sent these men to show man the right way of living. He raised each of them from amongst the people who they preached to. Thus, these men were of the same culture, nature, and civilization as the men whom they sought to guide. God gave them knowledge about the true meaning and purpose of life and of the life after death. He showed them the way that, if followed, would lead man to success and eternal happiness. These chosen men are the Messengers of God—His prophets. God communicated knowledge and wisdom to them by means of revelation, and the book containing the Divine Communications is called the Book of God, or the Word of God. Now the test of man's wisdom and intelligence lies in this: does he recognize God's Messenger after observing his pure and righteous life and after carefully studying his noble and flawless teachings? The man who possesses wisdom and common sense would verify truth and accept the instructions given by the Messenger of truth. If he denies the Messenger of God and his teachings, his denial would signify that he lacked the capacity to recognize truth and righteousness. Because of his denial, he would fail in his test. Such a man will never be able to discover the truth about God, His Law and life after death.

Faith in the Unknown

It is an everyday experience that when you do not know about something, you look for somebody who knows about it and trust his word and follow him. If you get sick and cannot treat yourself, you go to the doctor and accept and follow his instructions without question. Why? Because he is properly qualified to give medical advice, is experienced in the field, and has treated and cured a number of patients. So you stick to his advice, do whatever he asks you to do and avoid whatever he forbids. In matters of Law, you believe in whatever your legal adviser says and act accordingly. In educational matters you have faith in your teacher or professor and accept his instructions as true. When you want to go somewhere and do not know how to get there, you ask somebody who knows the way and follow the directions he gives you. In short, the reasonable course to adopt in all aspects of life concerning matters which you do not or cannot know is to approach one who knows about them, accept his advice, and act accordingly. Since your own knowledge of that matter is inadequate, you carefully search for one who knows and then silently accept his word. You take every pain to select the proper person. But after selecting the right man, you accept his advice without question. This kind of belief is called 'belief in the unknown'. For here you have relied upon one who knows in matters where you do not know. This putting of your faith in what was previously unknown to you is called '*faith in the unknown*'.

Faith in the unknown means that you accept the knowledge of what you don't know about from one who does know. You do not know about God and His true qualities. You are not aware that His angels are directing the machinery of the entire universe according to His commands, and that they surround you on all sides. You do not have the correct information about the way of life through which you can seek the pleasure of your Creator. And you are in the dark about the life that is to come. Knowledge about all these matters is given to you by the prophets. They had direct contact with Almighty God and were given correct knowledge by Him. They are the persons whose sincerity, integrity, truthfulness, and absolute purity of whose lives stands as undeniable witness to the truth of their claim to knowledge.

This conviction you have is *faith in the unknown (and unseen)*. In order to be obedient to God and live a life in agreement with His pleasure, a person must have this faith. He must be able to recognize and acknowledge truth. And there is no other medium besides God's Messenger to gain this true knowledge and thereby proceed correctly on the road of Islam.

CHAPTER THREE

THE PROPHETHOOD

Our earlier discussion outlined the following points:

1. The right course for man is to live in obedience to God, and for the observance of such a life, knowledge and faith are absolutely essential. It means one must have knowledge about God and His special qualities, His likes and dislikes, and one must know His chosen way and about the Day of Judgment. Then there must be unflinching faith in the truthfulness of this knowledge. This is *iman* (faith).

2. Secondly, God has graciously spared man the difficult task of acquiring this knowledge through his own effort alone. He has not put man to this difficult trial. Instead, He revealed this to the prophets. He commanded them to convey the Will of God to the people and show them the right path. This has saved man from tremendous anguish and adversity.

3. Lastly, the duty of all men and women is to recognize the prophet and follow in his footsteps. This is the road to salvation.

Now we will discuss the nature, history, and other aspects of prophethood.

I. Prophethood: Its Nature and Necessity

You can see that God was so kind and generous that He provided in this universe everything that man needs. Every newborn child arrives in the world gifted with eyes to see, ears to hear, nose to smell and breathe, hands to touch, feet to walk, and a mind to think and ponder.

Everything that a man needs, all the necessary abilities and resources are provided and marvelously set into his tiny body. Each and every minute requirement is foreseen and provided for, and nothing which he needs is left out.

The same is true for the world in which he lives. Everything essential for his life is provided in abundance—air, light, heat, water, and so on. The child, upon opening his eyes, finds food in his mother's breast. His parents have an instinctive love for him, and in their hearts has been implanted an irresistable urge to look after him, to bring him up and to sacrifice their all for his welfare. Under the sheltering care of the sustaining system which surrounds him, the child grows to maturity and can obtain the things he needs in every stage of his growth. In fact, all the material conditions needed for survival and growth are provided for and he finds that the whole universe is at his service, serving him at every turn and pass.

This is not all. Man is blessed with all those potentials and abilities — physical, mental, and moral — which he requires in his struggle for life. Here God has made a wonderful arrangement. He has not distributed these gifts to men strictly equally. Their equal distribution would have made men totally independent of each other and impaired the possibilities of mutual care and cooperation. Even though mankind on the whole possesses all that is needed, yet among men qualities and abilities are distributed unequally and sparingly. Some possess physical strength and athletic ability; others are noted for their mental talents. Some are born with greater talents for art, poetry, and philosophy while others possess military skill, speaking abilities, commercial intelligence, mathematical keeness, scientific curiosity, literary observation, etc. These special talents make a man distinct, and give him the ability to grasp those complex concepts which elude the grip of most individuals. These intuitions and talents are gifts from God. They are found naturally contained within those individuals who have been so distinguished by God.

Careful reflection upon this arrangement of God's gifts also reveals that the talents have been distributed among men in a marvelous way. Capacities which are essential for the general maintenance of human culture have been given to most human beings, while those extraordinary talents which are required on a limited scale are given only to a few. The number of soldiers, farmers, craftsmen, and laborers is large; but military generals, scholars, statesmen, and intellectuals are comparatively few. The same is true with all professions, arts, and sciences. The general rule seems to be: The higher the capacity and greater the genius, the lesser the number of people who possess them. Super-geniuses, who leave a mark on human history which cannot be erased, are few and far between. Their number is still less.

Here, we are faced with another question. Is the fundamental need of human culture confined to the need of experts and specialists in the fields of law and politics, science and mathematics, engineering and mechanics, finance and economics, or does it also need men who can show man the Right Path—the way to God and salvation? Other experts provide man with knowledge about all that is in this world and of the manner by which to use it. Yet there must be someone to tell man the purpose of creation and the meaning of life itself. Who is man and why has he been created? Who has provided him with his abilities and resources and why? What are the goals of life and how can they be attained? This is the most essential need of man and unless he knows this he cannot erect the edifice of culture on sound foundations and cannot succeed in life here and in the hereafter. Our reasoning refuses to believe that God Who has provided man with even the most trivial of his requirements would neglect to provide for this greatest and most vital need. In fact, it can never be so. And it is not so. While God produced men of distinction in arts and sciences, He has also raised men with deep vision, pure intuition, and the highest abilities to know and understand Him. He Himself revealed to them the way of godliness and righteousness. He gave them knowledge concerning the goals of life. He taught them the values of morality and entrusted them with the duty of communicating God's Revelation to other men to show them the Right Path. These men are prophets and messengers of God.

The prophets are distinguished from others in human society by their special talents, their natural mental outlook, and a pure and meaningful living, more-or-less in the same way that other geniuses in the arts and sciences are distinguished. The genius in a man is its own advertisement and automatically persuades others to recognize it. For instance, when we listen to a born poet, we can immediately detect his special talent. If those who don't have this ability try even their level best to gain poetic excellence, they cannot succeed. The same is true with a born speaker, writer, leader and inventor. Every such talent distinguishes itself by its remarkable ability and extraordinary achievements. Others cannot stand a match to it. The same is true of a prophet. His mind grasps problems which defy other minds; he speaks and throws rare lights on subjects on which no one else can speak. He gets insight into subtle and intricate questions that no one else would have understood even after years of deep thought and meditation. Reason accepts whatever he says; the heart feels its truth. The experiences and observations of things in this world all go to testify to the truth of every word that flows from his mouth. If, however, we ourselves try to produce the same or a similar work, nothing but failure meets us. His nature and character are so good and pure that in all affairs his attitude is that of truthfulness, straightforwardness, and nobility. He never does or utters wrong, nor does he commit any evil. He always inspires virtue and righteousness, and practices himself what he preaches to others. No incident of his life shows that his life is not in harmony with his ideal. Neither his word nor deed is prompted by any self-interest. He suffers for the good of others, and never makes others suffer for his own good. His whole life is an example of truth, nobleness, purity, high thinking; in fact, it is the most exalted form of human living. His character is without blemish and even the minutest scrutiny fails to reveal any flaw in his life. All these facts, all these qualities make it clear that he is the prophet of God and faith must be placed in him.

When it becomes clear that a certain person is the true prophet of God, the natural result of this realization is that his words should be accepted, his instructions followed, and his orders obeyed. It is unreasonable to accept a man as

God's true prophet, and yet not believe in what he says or not follow what he ordains. Your acceptance of him as God's prophet means you have acknowledged that what he says is from God Almighty and that whatever he does is in accordance with God's Will and Pleasure. Now, disobedience to him is the disobedience of God—and disobedience of God leads to nothing but ruin and devastation. Therefore, the very acceptance of the prophet makes it incumbent on you to bow to his instructions and accept them without any hesitation whatsoever. You may not be able to fully grasp the wisdom and usefulness of this or that order, but the fact that an instruction came from the prophet is sufficient guarantee for its truth. There can be no room for doubt or suspicion. Your inability to understand it is no reason for its having flaw or defect; a common man's understanding is not flawless. It has its limitations and they cannot be ignored altogether. It is clear that one who does not have a thorough knowledge about a certain thing cannot understand its refinements. But such a person would be a fool to reject what an expert says, merely on the plea that he himself does not fully understand the expert. In every important worldly affair an expert is needed for advice, and when you turn to the expert you thereafter trust his advice and entirely depend upon it. You surrender your own right of judgment and follow him honorably. Every ordinary man cannot be a master in all arts and crafts of the world. The proper way for an average human being is to do what he can and, in respect of things he cannot do, to use all his wisdom and shrewdness in finding the proper man to guide and help him, and after finding such a man, to accept his advice and follow him. When you are sure a certain person is the best man available for the job, you seek his advice and guidance, and have complete trust in him. To interfere with him at every step and say, "Make me understand it before you proceed any further", is obviously unnecessary. When you hire a lawyer for a legal case, you do not interfere with him on every turn and pass. Rather, you have faith in him and follow his advice. For your medical treatment you go to the doctor and follow his instructions. You neither poke your nose in medical matters nor test your skill in logic by debating with the doctor. This is the proper attitude in life. The same must be done in the case of religion. You need the knowledge of God; you need to know the system of life according to God's pleasure; and you possess no means for obtaining this knowledge. It is incumbent upon you, therefore, to look for a true prophet of God. You will have to use utmost care and intelligence in your search for him, and if you choose a wrong man for a true prophet, he will put you on the wrong track. If, however, after properly weighing all considerations, you decide without doubt that a certain person is really God's prophet, then you must trust him completely and obey all his instructions faithfully.

Now it is clear that the Right Path for man is that and that alone which the prophet declares to be so and the correct way of life is only that which he informs us to be from God. From this, one can easily understand that to have faith in the prophet and to obey and follow him is absolutely necessary for all men, and that a man who puts aside the prophet's instructions and tries to carve out a way for himself, deviates from the Right Path and surely goes astray.

In this matter, men are guilty of strange errors. There are men who admit the integrity and truthfulness of the prophet, but do not believe in him, nor do they follow him in the affairs of their life. Such men are not only unbelievers, but also behave in an arrogant and unnatural way. To not follow the prophet after admitting him to be true means that one knowingly follows untruth. And what foolishness can be greater than that!

Some people declare, "We do not need a prophet for our guidance and we can ourselves find the way to truth." This too is a faulty view. You have probably studied geometry, and you know that between two points there can be only one straight line. All other lines must be crooked or will fail to touch the point in question. The same is the case with the way to truth, which, in the language of Islam, is called the *Straight Path*. This path begins from man and goes straight towards God.

This path can obviously be one and only one; all other paths would be aberrations and would lead astray. This Straight Path has been illustrated by the prophet, and there is and can be no straight path besides it. The man who ignores it and seeks other ways is only a victim of his imagination. He chooses a way and imagines it to be right, but soon finds himself entangled, and is lost in the maze created by his fancy. What would you think of a person who has lost his way and when a good man shows him the right one, ignores the guidance, declaring "I will not take your guidance nor accept the way you have shown me, but I will grope in this unknown region and try to reach the objective of my search in my own way"? This, in the presence of clear guidance from the prophets, is sheer stupidity. If everybody tried to start up again by developing a system of divine guidance from scratch, it would be a gross waste of time and energy. We never do this in the field of sciences and arts, why here?

This is a common error, and a little thinking will reveal its flaws and weaknesses. If you reflect on this deeply, you will notice that a person who refuses to believe in the true prophet cannot find any way straight or otherwise to reach God. This is because a man who refuses to believe in the advice of a truthful man adopts such a perverse attitude that the prospects of truth become estranged from him. He thus becomes a victim of his own obstinance, arrogance, bias, and perversity. Often, his denial of truth is simply due to arrogance or a blind will to avoid change. It may be due to a stubborn desire to adhere to the way of the forefathers, or slavery of the lower desires whose gratification becomes impossible by obedience to the teachings of the prophets. If a man is engrossed in any of the above conditions, the path of truth becomes closed to him. He, like a jaundiced person, cannot look upon things in the uncolored light of reality. Such a man cannot discover any road to salvation. On the other hand, if a man is sincere and truth-loving, if he is not a slave to any of the above conditions, the road to reality becomes paved for him. There are absolutely no grounds for him to refuse to believe in the prophet and to follow him. In fact, he finds in the teachings of the prophet the very echo of his soul and discovers himself by discovering the prophet.

And, above all, the true Prophet is raised by God Himself. It is He Who sent him to mankind to convey His message to the people. It is His Command for man to put its faith in the prophet and follow him. Thus, one who refuses to believe in God's Messenger actually refuses to follow God's Commandments and becomes a rebel. There is no denying that one who refuses to acknowledge the authority of the deputy of a sovereign actually refuses the authority of the sovereign himself. This disobedience turns him into a rebel. God is the Lord of the universe, the true Sovereign, the King of Kings, and it is the absolute duty of every man to acknowledge the authority of His Messengers and Apostles. Man must obey them as His accredited prophets. And one who turns away from the prophet of God is surely a tyrant, be he a believer in God or a disbeliever.

II

BRIEF HISTORY OF PROPHETHOOD

Now, let's glance at the history of prophethood. Let us see how this long chain began, how it gradually unfolded itself and finally culminated in the prophethood of the last of the prophets, Muhammad (peace be upon him).

The human race began from one man: Adam. It was from him that the family of man grew and the human race multiplied. All human beings born in this world have descended from the earliest pair: Adam and Eve. History and religion agree on this point. Scientific investigations about the origin of man also do not show that originally, different men came into existence simultaneously or at different points of time in different parts of the world. In fact, most scientists theorize that one man was brought into existence first, and the entire human race probably descended from that same one man.

Adam, the first man on earth, was also appointed as the first Prophet of God. God revealed his religion — Islam —

to him and told him to convey and communicate it to his descendents. He was to teach them that God is One, the Creator, the Sustainer of the world, that He is the Lord of the universe and He alone should be worshipped and obeyed. He was to make it clear that to Him they will have to return one day and to Him alone they should appeal for help and that they should live good, pious and righteous lives in accordance with God's pleasure. If they did this, they would be blessed by God with tremendous rewards. If they turned away and disobeyed Him they would be losers here and in the hereafter, and would be severely punished for their disbelief and disobedience.

The descendents of Adam who were good walked the right path shown to them by him. Those who were bad abandoned their father's teachings, and gradually drifted away into devious ways. Some began to worship the sun, the moon, and the stars. Others worshipped trees, animals, and rivers. Some believed that air, water, fire, health, and the rest of the forces of Nature were each under the control of a different god and that each god should be pacified by means of worship. In this way, ignorance gave rise to many forms of polytheism[1] and idolatry, and scores of religions were created. This was the age when Adam's offspring spread all over the globe, and formed different races and nations. Every nation made a different religion for itself, each with practices and rituals of its own. God — the one Master and Creator of mankind and the universe — was altogether forgotten. Not only that, Adam's descendants forgot even the way of life which God revealed directly for them and which their great father taught them. Rather they followed their own desires. Every kind of evil custom grew; and all sorts of ignorant ideas spread among the people. They began to err in distinguishing right from wrong. Many evils were considered proper while many right things were not only ignored but dubbed as wrong.

At this stage, God began to raise prophets among every people. Each prophet reminded his people of the lesson they had forgotten. They taught the worship of One God,

---

[1] Polytheism means the worship of many gods.

put an end to idol worship and to the practice of associating other gods with God. All customs of ignorance were removed by them, and the people were taught the right way of living, a living which would bring them the pleasure of Almighty God. Pure and Godly laws were given to them, laws which were to be followed and enforced into society. God's true prophets were raised in all countries, in every land and among every people. They all possessed the same religion — the religion of Islam. No doubt, the methods of teaching and the legal system of each prophet differed slightly according to the needs of the people, or according to the stage in which the culture of the people was at that time. The particular teachings of each prophet were determined by the kind of evils which he faced and sought to eradicate. The methods of reform differed as suited to fight different notions and ideas. When people were in primitive stages of society, civilization, and intellectual development, their laws and rules were simple. These laws were modified and improved as the society evolved and progressed. However, these differences were obvious and their importance was superficial. The fundamental teachings of all the religions were the same, i.e. belief in the Oneness of God, adherence to a life of goodness and peace, and belief in life after death with its just mechanism for reward and punishment.

Man's attitude towards God's prophets has been strange. First, he maltreated the prophets and refused to listen to or accept their teachings. Some prophets were expelled from their homelands, while some were assassinated. Others, faced by the people's indifference, continued preaching for their entire lives, and won only a few followers. In the midst of the harrassing opposition, ridicule and resentment to which they were continuously subjected, these prophets of God did not cease to preach. The foolish and erroneous ways of the people, which were the result of centuries of persistence in deviation, ignorance, and wrongdoing, now took another form. Though the people accepted and practiced their teachings while their prophets were alive, after their deaths they introduced distorted concepts of their past. They put these distorted and senseless ideas into their religions thereby altering the prophet's teachings. The pure source of knowledge of God, Most High was now polluted by their ignorance. Novel methods for worshipping God were developed. Some even decided to worship their prophets as gods. Some made their prophets the sons of God while others associated their Messengers with God in his Divinity. In short, the various behaviors of man in this respect were a travesty of all reason and a mockery of himself. He made idols of those very persons whose mission was to smash idols to pieces. By intermixing religion, customs, foolish rituals, baseless and false stories, and legends and man-made laws, men changed and perverted the teachings of the prophets so much that after a lapse of centuries, it became confusing as to what was real and what was fictitious. The teachings of the prophets were lost in a mess of fictions and perversities so much so that it became impossible to distinguish the grain from the chaff. Not content with corrupting the prophets' teachings, they further ascribed false tales and derogatory traditions to the lives of the prophets. By all these things, the prophets' life histories became so polluted that a real and reliable account of their lives became impossible to discern. Despite these corruptions, the work of the prophets has not been totally in vain. Among all nations, in spite of corruptions and alterations, some traces of Truth have survived. The idea of God and of the life after death was definitely assimilated in some form or other. A few principles of goodness, truthfulness and morality were commonly admitted throughout the world. The prophets thus prepared the minds of their people in such a way that a universal religion could be safely introduced — a religion which is fully in agreement with the nature of man. They prepared man's mind for that universal religion which embodies all that was good in all other creeds and societies, and which is acceptable to the entire human race.

As we have said above, in the beginning separate prophets used to appear among different nations or groups of people. The teachings of each prophet were meant specifically for his people. The reason was that at that stage of history, nations were situated separately and were so cut off from each other that people were isolated within the geographical limits of their territories. Also, facilities for intercommunication were non-existent. Under these circumstances, it was very difficult to propagate a common World Faith with its accompanying system of law for how we should live in this world. Besides, the general conditions of the early nations differed widely from one another. Their ignorance was great, which caused the different peoples to have developed various forms of moral deviations. Because of this, it was necessary that different prophets be raised to preach the Truth to them and win them over to God's ways. It was necessary for them to gradually eradicate evils and deviations; to root out the ways of ignorance and teach them to practice the noblest principles of a simple and righteous life. By so doing they would ultimately train and bring them up in the skills and trades of life. God alone knows how many thousands of years were spent in educating man in this manner, and in developing him mentally, morally, and spiritually. Man continued to make progress and at last the time came when he emerged from his infancy, and entered the age of maturity.

With progress and the spread of trade, industry, and arts, communication was established between nations. From China and Japan, as far as the distant reaches of Europe and Africa, routes were opened by both land and sea. Many learned the art of writing and knowledge spread. Ideas began to be communicated from one country to another and learning and scholarship began to be exchanged. Great conquerors appeared, extended their conquests far and wide, and established vast empires. They knit together many different nations under one political system. Thus, nations came closer and their differences diminished.

It became possible, under these circumstances, that one system presenting a comprehensive life be sent. The conditions demanded that a system catering to the moral, spiritual, social, cultural, political, economic and all other needs of men; one containing both religious and secular elements be sent by the All-Knowing God. It demanded that this system be sent for all mankind. More than 2,000 years ago, mankind attained a mental status which indicated that it craved a universal religion. Buddhism, though consisting of only a few moral principles and not a complete system of life, emerged from India and spread as far as Japan and Mongolia on one side, and Afghanistan and Russia on the other. Its missionaries travelled far and wide in the world. A few centuries later Christianity appeared. Although the religion taught by Jesus Christ (peace be on him) was none but Islam, his followers reduced it to a religion called Christianity, and even this well-known and Israelized religion spread to the far reaches of Persia and Asia Minor, and into the distant lands of Europe and Africa. One can clearly conclude from these events that the conditions of mankind at that time demanded a common religion for the whole human race. In fact, they were so prepared for it that when they found no complete and true religion in existence, they began to propagate the prevalent religions, no matter how defective, incomplete, or unsatisfying they were.

At such a crucial stage of civilization, when man's mind was craving a world religion, a prophet was raised in Arabia. The religion he was given to propagate was again Islam — but now in the form of a complete, full-fledged system covering all aspects of the individual and material life. He was made a prophet for the entire human race and was deputed to propagate his mission to the whole world. He was Muhammad, the Prophet of Islam (peace be on him).

THE PROPHETHOOD OF MUHAMMAD

If we look at the world atlas, we find that no other country could have been more suitable for the much needed world religion than Arabia. It is located right in the middle of Asia and Africa, and Europe is not far away from it. At the time of Muhammad's appearance, the central part of Europe was inhabited by civilized and culturally advanced nations. Thus, these people were at about the same distance from Arabia as were the people of India. This fact gave Arabia a central position.

Look at the history of that era and you will find that no other people were more suited to be given his prophethood than the Arabs.

Great nations of the world were struggling hard to gain world supremacy, and in this long and ceaseless struggle, they exhausted all their resources and vitality. The Arabs were a fresh and virile people. The so-called social progress produced bad habits among the advanced nations, while among the Arabs no such social organization existed. They were, therefore, free from the inactivity, debasement and indulgences arising out of luxury and sensual satiety. The pagan Arabs of the fifth century had not been affected by the evil influence of the artificial social systems and civilization of the great nations of the world. They possessed all the good human qualities which a people untouched by the 'social progress' of that time ought to possess. They were brave, fearless, generous and were faithful to their promises. Lovers of freedom, they were politically independent, not being subject to the jurisdiction of any of the imperial powers. They lived a simple life, and were strangers to the life of luxury and indulgence. No doubt, there were certain undesirable aspects of their lives as well, as we shall mention later on. But the reason for the existence of these aspects was that for thousands of years no prophet had risen among them. Nor had there appeared a reformer who might have civilized them and purged their life of all evil impurities. Centuries of independent life in sandy deserts had bred and nourished extreme ignorance among them. They had become so hard-hearted and firm in their ignorant traditions that to make them human again was not the task of an ordinary man. However, they did possess a capacity that if some person of extraordinary powers were to invite them to reform and gave them a noble goal to reach and a complete program by which to reach it, they would accept his call. They would readily rise to act for the achievement of such a goal, and spare no suffering or sacrifice in the cause. They would even be prepared to face without the least bit of hesitation the hostility of the entire world in the cause of their mission. And clearly it was such a young, forceful, and virile people that were needed for propagating the teachings of the World Prophet, Muhammad (peace be on him).

And then look at the Arabic language. If you study it and probe deeply into its literature, you will be convinced that there is no language other than Arabic which is more suited to give expression to high ideals, to explain the most delicate and intricate issues of Divine knowledge. No language other than Arabic could so effectively impress the heart of man and mold it into submission to God. Small phrases and brief sentences express a world of ideas, and at the same time are so forceful that they steal into the depths of the heart. Their very sound moves men to tears and ecstasy. They are so sweet that it feels as if honey were being poured into the ears. So full of harmony are they that every tissue of the listener's body is moved by their symphony. It is such a rich and powerful language that was needed for the Qur'an, the Great Word of God.

It was therefore a demonstration of the great wisdom of Almighty God that He chose the land of Arabia for the birth place of the World Prophet. Let us now see how unique and extraordinary was the blessed personality chosen by God for this mission.

III

MUHAMMAD'S PROPHETHOOD: A RATIONAL VINDICATION

If one were to close his eyes and imagine himself in the world of 1400 years ago, he would find that it was a world completely different from the one we live in. He would not find the slightest resemblance to the environment we find ourselves in today. How few and far between were the opportunities for the exchange of ideas! How limited and primitive were the means of communication! How minute and meager was man's knowledge and narrow was his outlook. How enveloped was he in superstition and how uncivilized and uncouth was his thinking.

Darkness held the sway. There was only a faint glimmer of learning which could hardly brighten the horizon of human knowledge. There were no radios, telephones, televisions, or cinemas. Railroads, automobiles, and airplanes were undreamt of and printing presses and publishing houses were unknown. Hand-written books and copies thereof alone supplied whatever scanty literary material there was. Education was regarded as a luxury meant only for the most fortunate, and educational institutions were few and far between.

The store of human knowledge was scanty, man's outlook was narrow, and his ideas concerning life were confined to his limited surroundings. Even a scholar of that age lacked in certain respects the knowledge possessed by a layman of today, and the most cultured person was less refined than our own man in the street.

Indeed, humanity was steeped in the extremes of ignorance and superstition. Whatever light of learning there was seemed to be fighting a losing battle against the darkness which prevailed all around. What are considered to be matters of common knowledge today could hardly be acquired then, even after years of intense thought and research. Things which we now classify as 'myth' and 'superstition' were then regarded as unquestionable truths. Acts which we now deem savage and barbarous were for them the order of the day. Methods which we would now clearly recognize as repulsive and degrading were the very soul of their morality, and people couldn't imagine in those days that there could be a different way of life besides this.

Skepticism had reached such mighty proportions that people refused to consider anything as lofty and sublime unless it appeared in the form of the supernatural, the extraordinary, the uncanny, and even the illogical. They developed such a distorted mentality that they could never imagine a human being to possess a godly soul nor the saint to be human.

ARABIA — The Abyss of Darkness

In that era of ignorance, there was a country where darkness lay even thicker. The neighboring countries of Persia, Byzantium, and Egypt possessed at least a glimmer of civilization and a faint light of learning. But Arabia could receive no share of their cultural influences. It stood isolated, cut off by vast oceans of sand. Arab traders plodded great distances for months at a time just to carry their goods to and from these countries. They could hardly acquire any bits of knowledge on their journeys. In their country, there wasn't a single educational institution. There were no libraries, and books were rare treasures. No one seemed interested in the production and advancement of knowledge. The few who could read were not educated enough to be in any way involved with the existing arts and sciences. They did possess a highly developed language which was capable of expressing the finest qualities of human thought in a remarkable manner. Their literary taste was also of a high degree. But a study of the remnants of their literature reveals how limited was their knowledge, how low were their standards of culture and civilization, how saturated were their minds with superstitions, how barbarous and ferocious were their thoughts and customs, and how uncouth and degraded were their conceptions of morality.

It was a country without a government. Every tribe claimed authority and considered itself to be an independent unit. In fact, there was no law except the law of the jungle. Loot, arson, and murder of innocent and weak was the order of the day. Life, property, and honor were constantly at stake. Different tribes were always at swords drawn against one another. Any trivial incident was enough to cause a war to burst out in ferocious fury which sometimes even developed into a country-wide conflict lasting for several decades.

Whatever notions they had of morals, culture, and civilization were primitive and uncouth. They could hardly discriminate between pure and impure, lawful and unlawful, civil and uncivil. Their life was wild. Their methods

40

were barbaric. They took pleasure in adultery, gambling, and drinking. Loot and plunder was their motto, murder and raping their habits. They would stand stark naked before each other without any qualms of conscience. Even their women would become naked at the ceremony of going around the mosque in Mecca. Out of sheer foolish notions of prestige, they would bury their daughters alive lest anyone should become their son-in-law. They would marry their step-mothers after the death of their fathers. They were even ignorant in elements of everyday routine such as eating, dressing, and washing.

Concerning their religious beliefs, they suffered from the same evils which were playing havoc with the rest of the world.

They worshipped stones, trees, idols, stars, and spirits; in short, everything conceivable except God. They did not know anything about the teachings of the prophets of old. They understood that Abraham and Ishmael were their forefathers, but they knew next to nothing about their religious teachings or about the God whom these prophets worshipped. The stories of Ad and Thamud were found in their folklore, but they contained no traces of the teachings of prophets Hud and Salih. The Jews and Christians transmitted certain legendary folktales to them about the Israelite prophets. However, these stories presented a terrible picture of those noble souls. They adulterated their teachings with figments of their imagination and tarred their lives black. Indeed, the picture presented in these traditions about the institution of prophethood and of the character of the Israelite prophets is exactly the opposite of all that these noble followers of truth stood for.

The Savior is Born

In such a dark age and in such an ignorant country, a man was born. In his early childhood, his parents died. He was left with his grandfather, who a few years later died as well. Consequently, he was deprived of even the scant training and upbringing which an Arab child normally received. In his boyhood, he tended flocks of sheep and goats in the presence of bedouin youth. When he was old enough, he became a businessman. All his associations and dealings were with the Arabs alone, whose sorry state has just been described. Education had not even touched him, he was completely unlettered and unschooled. He could neither read nor write, and he never got a chance to sit in the company of learned men, for such men were totally non-existent in Arabia at that time. He did have a few opportunities to go out of his country, but those journeys were business trips undertaken by Arab trade caravans. If he met any learned men or had the occasion to observe any aspects of culture and civilization, those random meetings and stray observations couldn't be given any place in the making of his personality. Such things can never have that profound influence on anyone which would lift him totally out of his environment so that he has no similarity with it. They can never transform him completely, and raise him to such heights of originality and glory that there remains no likeness between him and the society in which he is born. Nor can they be the manner by which that profound and vast knowledge is acquired which would transform the unlettered Bedouin into a leader not only of his country and age, but of the world at large for all ages to come. Indeed, whatever the effect the intellectual and cultural influence of those journeys one might suppose, the fact remains that they could in no way impart to him those conceptions and principles of religion, ethics, culture, and civilization which were totally nonexistent in the world at that time. And they could not have created that sublime and perfect pattern of human character which was then nowhere to be found.

Diamond in a Heap of Stones

We can now look at the life and work of this noble man in the context not only of Arabian society, but also of the entire world as it stood then.

He is totally different from the people among whom he is born and with whom he spends his youth and early manhood. He never tells a lie. The whole nation is unanimous in testifying to his truthfulness. Even his worst enemies never accuse him of telling a lie on any occasion whatsoever during his entire life. He talks politely and never uses obscene and abusive language. He has such a charming personality and such winsome manners, that he captivates the hearts of those who come into contact with him. In his dealings with people, he always follows the principles of justice and fairplay. He remains engaged in business and trade for years, but he never enters into any dishonest transaction. Those who deal with him in business have full confidence in his integrity. The entire nation calls him "the Truthful and the Truthworthy". Even his enemies deposit their costly belongings with him for safe custody and he equitably fulfills this trust. He is the very embodiment of modesty in the midst of a society which is immodest to the core. Born and bred among a people who regard drunkenness and gambling as virtues, he never touches alcohol and never indulges in gambling. His people are uncouth, uncultured and unclean, but personified in him is the highest culture and the most refined, aesthetic outlook. Surrounded on all sides by heartless people, he himself has a heart overflowing with the milk of human kindness. He helps the orphans and widows. He is hospitable to travelers. He harms no one; rather, he goes all out to suffer hardships for others' sake. Living among those for whom war is bread and butter, he is such a lover of peace that his heart melts for them when they take up arms and cut each other's throats. He keeps aloof from the feuds of his tribe, and is foremost in bringing about reconciliation. Brought up in an idolatrous society, he is so clear-minded and possesses such a pure soul that he regards nothing in the heavens and the earth worthy of worship except the One True God. He does not bow before any created thing and does not partake in the offerings made to idols, even in his childhood. Instinctively, he hates all kind of worship of all creatures besides God. In brief, the towering and radiant personality of *this man,* in the midst of such a corrupted and dark environment, may be likened to a beacon-light brightening a pitch-dark night or to a diamond in a heap of dead stones.

A Revolution Comes

After spending his life in such a chaste, pure, and civilized manner, there comes a revolution in his being. He feels fed up with the darkness and ignorance, corruption, immorality, idolatry, and disorder which surround him on all sides. He finds everything around him out of harmony with his soul. He retires to the hills, away from humdrum of society. He spends days and nights in perfect seclusion and meditation. He fasts so that his soul and heart may become purer and nobler still.

He thinks and ponders deep. He is in search of the light which might melt away the surrounding darkness. He wants to get hold of that power with which he might bring about the downfall of the corrupt and disorderly world and lay the foundations of a new and better one.

Lo! a remarkable revolution overcomes his person. All of a sudden his heart is illuminated with the Divine Light giving him the power he had yearned for. He comes out of the confinement of his cave, goes to the people, and addresses them in the following strain:

"The idols which you worship are a mere sham. Cease to worship them from now onward. No mortal being, no star, no tree, no stone, no spirit, is worthy of human worship. Therefore, bow not your heads in worship before them. The entire universe with everything that it contains belongs to God Almighty alone. He alone is the Creator, the Nourisher, the Sustainer, and, consequently, the real Sovereign before Whom all should bow down and to Whom all should pray and render obedience. Thus worship Him alone and obey only His commands. Loot and plunder, murder and rape, injustice and cruelty — all the vices in which you indulge are crimes in the eyes of God. Leave your evil ways. He hates them all. Speak the truth. Be just. Do not kill anyone. Do not rob anyone. Take your lawful share. Give what is due to others in a just manner. You are human beings and all human beings are equal in the eyes of God. None is born with the slur of shame on his face, nor anyone has come into the world with the mantle of honor hung around his neck. He alone is high and honored who is God-fearing and pious, true in words and deeds. Distinctions of birth and glory of race are no measure of greatness and honor. One who fears God and does good deeds is the noblest of human beings. One who has no love for Almighty God and is steeped in bad manners is doomed. There is an appointed day after your death when you shall have to appear before your Lord. You shall be called to account for all your deeds, good or bad, and you shall not be able then to hide anything. The whole record of your life shall be an open book to Him. Your fate shall be determined by your good or bad actions. In the court of the True Judge — the all-seeing and knowing God — the question of unfair recommendation and favoritism does not arise. You shall not be able to bribe Him. No consideration will be given to your family status or history. True faith and good deeds alone will put you in good standing at that time. He who will be fully equipped with them shall take his abode in the Heaven of eternal happiness, while one devoid of them shall be cast in the fire of Hell."

This is the message with which he comes. The ignorant nation turns against him. Abuses and stones are showered at his august person. Every conceivable torture and cruelty is perpetrated on him; and this continues not for a day or two but ceaselessly for thirteen long, troublesome years. At last he is exiled. But he is not given intermission from persecution even there. He is tormented in various ways in his home of refuge. The whole of Arabia is incited against him. He is persecuted and hounded down continuously for eight full years there. He suffers it all, but does not budge an inch from the stand he has taken. He is resolute, firm, and inflexible in his stance and purpose.

Why all the Enmity (Hostility)?

One might inquire: Why did his nation become his sworn enemy? Was there any dispute about gold and silver or any other worldly possession? Was it due to any blood-feud? Did he ask for anything from them? No! All this hostility was based on the fact that he asked them to worship the One True God and to lead a life of righteousness, purity, and goodness. He preached against idolatry, told them not to worship other beings besides God, and denounced their wrong ways of living. He cut at the roots of priestcraft. He spoke against the distinctions of high and low between human beings, and condemned the prejudices of tribe and race as sheer ignorance. He wanted to change the whole structure of society which had been handed down to them from time immemorial. In their turn, his countrymen told him that the principles of his mission were hostile to their ancestral traditions and asked him either to give them up or bear the worst consequences.

One might ask: for what reason did he suffer all those hardships? His nation offered to accept him as their king and to lay all the riches of the land at his feet if only he would leave the preaching of his religion and spreading of his message. But he chose to refuse their tempting offers and to suffer for his cause instead. Why? Was he to gain in any way if those people changed their lives and became godly and righteous?

Why was it that he cared not a bit for riches and luxury, kingship and glory, and ease and plenty? Was he playing for some higher material gains so that these blessings sank into insignificance in comparison with them? Were those gains so tempting that he could elect to go through fire and sword and bear tortures of the soul and torments of body with unwavering composure for years? One has to ponder over it deeply to find an answer.

Can anyone ever imagine a higher example of self-sacrifice, brotherliness and kind-heartedness towards his fellow beings than that a man would ruin his happiness for the good of others, while those very people for whose betterment he is striving should stone him, abuse him, banish him, and give him no quarter even in his exile, and that, in spite of this all, he should refuse to stop working for their well-being?

46

Can any insincere person undergo so much suffering for a false cause? Can any dishonest speculator and visionary exhibit such firmness and determination for his ideal as to stick to his guns to the very last and remain unruffled in the face of dangers and tortures of every type when a whole country rises up in arms against him?

This faith, this firm commitment, and this resolution, with which he led his movement to ultimate success is, therefore, clear proof of the supreme truth of his cause. Had there been even the slightest doubt and uncertainty in his heart, he could never have been able to brave the storm which continued in all its fury for twenty-one long years.

This is one side of the revolution wrought in his being. The other is even more wonderful and remarkable.

A Changed Man at Forty—Why?

For forty years he lived as an Arab among Arabs. In all that time, he was not known as a statesman, a preacher, or an orator. None heard him imparting gems of wisdom and knowledge as he began to do thereafter. He was never seen discussing the principles of metaphysics, ethics, law, politics, economics, and sociology. Not to speak of being a great general, he was not even known as an ordinary soldier. He uttered no word about God, the Angels, the Revealed Books, the early Prophets, the bygone nations, the Day of Judgment, the Life after Death, Hell and Heaven. No doubt he possessed an excellent character and charming manners, and was highly cultured. Yet, there was nothing so deeply striking and so radically extraordinary in him which could make men expect something great and revolutionary from him in the future. He was known among people as a quiet, calm, gentle, law-abiding citizen of good nature. But when he came out of the cave with a new message, he was completely transformed.

When he began preaching his Message, all of Arabia stood in awe and wonder and was bewitched by his wonderful eloquence and oratory. It was so impressive and captivating that his worst enemies were afraid of hearing it, lest it should penetrate deep into the recesses of their hearts and carry them off their feet making them bid good-bye to their old religion and culture. It was so matchless that the whole legion of Arab poets, preachers, and speakers of the highest caliber failed to bring forth its equivalent. They failed to equal it even when he challenged his opponents to put their heads together and produce even a single line like the ones he recited.

His All-embracing Message

Now he appeared before his people as a unique philosopher, wonderful reformer and a renowned molder of culture and civilization. He came before them as an illustrious politician, a great leader, a judge of the highest eminence, and an incomparable general. This unlettered bedouin, this dweller of the desert, spoke with wisdom the like of which none had said before and none could say after. He expounded the intricate problems of metaphysics and theology. He delivered speeches on the principles of the decline and fall of nations and empires, supporting his thesis with historical data of the past. He reviewed the achievements of the reformers of old, passed judgments on the various religions, and gave verdicts on the differences and disputes between nations. He taught laws of ethics and principles of culture. He presented such laws of culture, economics, group conduct, and international relations that even eminent thinkers and scholars can grasp their true wisdom only after life-long research and experience. Their beauties, indeed, unfold themselves as man advances in theoretical knowledge and practical experience.

This silent and peace-loving trader who had never before handled a sword, who had no military training, who had but once participated in a battle and that too just as a spectator, turned into such a brave soldier that he did not even once retreat in the fiercest battles. He became such a great general that he conquered the entire Arabian peninsula in nine years at a time when the weapons were primitive and the means of communication poorest. His military skill and proficiency developed to such a height

48

and the military spirit and training he infused to a motley crowd of Arabs (who had no equipment worth the name) wrought such a miracle that within a few years they overthrew the two most formidable military powers of the day and became the masters of the then known world.

This reserved and quiet man who, for a full forty years, never gave any indication of political interest or activity, suddenly appeared on the stage of the world as such a great political reformer and statesman that without the aid of radio, telephone and press, he brought together the scattered inhabitants of a desert of twelve hundred thousand square miles. He joined together a people who were warlike, ignorant, unruly, uncultured, and plunged in self-destructive tribal warfare—under one banner, one law, one religion, one culture, one civilization, and one form of government.

He changed their ways of thinking, their very habits and morals. He turned the uncouth into the cultured, the barbarous into the civilized, the evil-doers and bad characters into God-fearing and righteous persons. Their unruly and stiff-necked natures were transformed into models of obedience to law and order. A nation which for centuries had produced not even a single great man worth the name, gave birth, under his influence and guidance, to thousands of noble souls who went to far-off corners of the world to preach and teach the principles of religion, morality, and civilization.

He accomplished this feat not through any lure, oppression or cruelty, but by his captivating manners, his winsome personality, and his convincing teachings. With his noble and gentle behavior, he befriended even his enemies. He captured the hearts of the people with his boundless sympathy and the milk of human kindness. He ruled justly. He did not swerve from truth and righteousness. He did not oppress even his deadly enemies who wanted to kill him, who pelted him with stones, who turned him out of his homeland, who pitched the whole of Arabia against him—nay, even those who chewed the raw liver of his dead uncle in a frenzy of vengeance.[1] He forgave them all when he triumphed over them. He never took revenge on anyone for his personal grievances. He did not retaliate against anyone for the wrongs perpetrated against him.

Despite the fact that he became the ruler of his country, he cared so little about himself and was so modest that he remained very simple and sparing in his habits. He lived poorly, as before, in his humble thatched-mud cottage. He slept on a mattress, wore coarse clothes, ate the simplest food, and sometimes went without food at all. He used to spend whole nights standing in prayer before his Master. He came to the rescue of the destitute and the penniless. He felt not the least reservation in working as a laborer. Till his last moments there was not the slightest tinge of kingly pomp and show nor arrogance of the mighty and the rich in him. Like an ordinary man, he would sit and walk with the people and share their joys and sorrows. He would so mix and mingle with the crowd that a stranger, an outsider, would find it difficult to point out the leader of the people and ruler of the nation from the rest of the company. Despite his greatness, his behavior with the meekest person was that of an ordinary man. Throughout his entire life he did not seek any reward or profit for himself or leave any property for his heirs. He dedicated his all to his people. He did not ask his followers to earmark anything for him or his descendants, so much so that he forbade his relatives from receiving the benefit of *zakat*[2] lest his followers at any future time hand out the whole share of it to them.

His Contribution to Human Thought

The achievements of this great man do not end here. In order to arrive at a correct appraisal of his true worth,

---

[1] Hamza, the uncle of the prophet, was slain during the battle of Uhad fought against the pagan Arabs. His chest was cut open and Hind, the wife of the chief of the pagans, actually tore out and chewed Hamza's liver.

[2] See page 103

one must look at it in the background of the history of the world as a whole. This would reveal that this unlettered dweller of the Arabian desert, who was born in the 'dark ages' over 1400 years ago, was the real pioneer of the modern age and the true leader of humanity. He is not only the leader of those who accept his leadership but also of those who do not acclaim him as such. He is even the leader of those who denounce him!—the only difference being they are unaware of the fact that his guidance is still imperceptibly influencing their thoughts and actions, and is the governing principle of their lives and the very spirit of modern times.

It was he who turned the course of human thought from love for superstition, the unnatural and unexplainable, towards a logical approach illustrating a love for truth and a balanced worldly life. It was he who, in a world which regarded only supernatural events as miracles and demanded their occurrence for verifying the truth of a religious mission, inspired the urge for rational proof as the criterion of truth. It was he who opened the eyes of those who were before accustomed to look for signs of God only in natural phenomena. It was he who, in the place of baseless speculation, led man to use logic and reasoning on the basis of observation, experimentation, and research. He was the one who clearly defined the limits and functions of sense perception, reason, and intuition. It was he who brought about a union between the spiritual and material values. It was he who harmonized Faith with Knowledge and Action. Joining scientific spirit with the power of religion, he was the first to unite these disciplines for the establishment of a better and more prosperous world.

He was the one who completely irradicated idolatry, man-worship, and the worship of many gods and replaced it with belief in One God. He was so thorough in this that even those religions which were based entirely on superstitions and idolatry were compelled to adopt a monotheistic theme. It was he who revolutionized the basic concepts of ethics and spirituality. To those who believed that asceticism and self-annihilation alone form the standard of moral and spiritual purity—that purity could not be achieved except by running away from life, disregarding the urges of the flesh and subjecting the body to all kinds of tortures—it was he who showed that spiritual evolution and salvation is attained through active participation in the practical affairs of this world.

It was he who showed man his true worth and position. Those who acknowledge only a God-incarnate or a son of God as their spiritual guide were told that human beings like themselves who don't claim to be gods can become the representative of God on earth. Those who proclaim kings and tyrants or other powerful individuals as their gods were made to understand that their false lords were mere ordinary human beings and nothing more. It was he who stressed that no man could claim holiness, authority, or kingship as his birthright—none were born with the brand of untouchability, slavery, or serfdom. He was the one whose example and teachings inspired the thoughts of the oneness of mankind, equality of the human race, true democracy and real freedom into the world.

In practical life, the results irreversibly impressed on the laws and ways of the world through the leadership of this illiterate person are countless. So many principles of culture, civilization, good behavior, and pure thinking prevalent in the world today owe their origin to him. The social laws he initiated have infiltrated deep into the structure of human social life, and this process continues up to this day. The economic principles he taught stimulated many movements in world history and hold out the same promise for the future. The laws of government he constructed revolutionized many of the political theories of the world and continue to project their influence even today. The basic principles of law and justice which bear the stamp of his genius had a remarkable influence on the administration of justice in the courts of nations. They form a perpetual source of guidance for all legislators and for all times to come. This unlettered Arab was the person who set on foot for the first time practically the whole framework of international relations. He regulated the laws for war and peace. No one previously had even the remotest idea that there could be an ethical code of war and that relations between different nations could be regulated on a common ground for the good of all mankind.

The Greatest Revolutionary

In the cavalcade of world history, the sublime figure of this wonderful person towers so high above all the great men of all times that they appear to be dwarfs when contrasted to him. Those who were famous as heroes of nations cannot be compared to him. None of them possessed a genius capable of making a deep impression on more than one or two aspects of life. Some are the exponents of theories and ideas but are deficient in practical action. Others are men of action but suffer from lack of knowledge. Some are renowned as statesmen only, others are masters of strategy and maneuvering. Some concentrated on one aspect of life in such a way that other aspects were overlooked. Some devoted their energies to ethical and spiritual values, but ignored economics and politics. Others concentrated on economics and politics, but neglected the spiritual side of life. In short, one comes across heroes who are experts in one walk of life only. His is the only example where all the excellences are blended together into one personality. He is a philosopher and a seer and also a living example of what he teaches. He is a great statesman as well as a military genius. He is a legislator and also a teacher of morals. He is a spiritual luminary as well as a religious guide. His vision penetrates every aspect of life and there is nothing which he touches and does not adorn. His orders and commandments cover a vast field from the regulation of international relations to the habits of everyday life like eating, drinking, and cleanliness of the body. On the foundations of his theories, he established a civilization and developed a culture. Herein he produced such a fine equilibrium in the conflicting aspects of life that one cannot find even the slightest trace of any flaw or defect. Can anyone point out any other example of such a perfect and all-around personality?

Most famous personalities are said to be products of their environment. But his case is unique. His environment seems to have played no part in the making of his personality. It also cannot be proved that historically his birth synchronized with what was occurring in Arabia at that time. The most one can say is that the circumstances in Arabia cried loud for the appearance of a person who could weld together the warring tribes into one nation and lay the foundation of their economic solidarity and well being by bringing other countries under their sway. In short, a national leader who had all the traits of an Arab of those days. A man who, through cruelty, oppression, bloodshed, deceit, and hypocrisy, or any other means fair or foul, could have enriched his people, conquered other nations, and left a kingdom as a heritage for his successors. One cannot prove any other crying need for the history of Arabia at that time.

In respect to Hegel's philosophy of history or Marx's historical materialism, the most that can be said is that the time and environment demanded the emergence of a leader who could create a nation and build an empire. But Hegel's and Marx's philosophy cannot explain how an environment like this could produce a man whose mission was to teach the best of morals, to purify humanity of all filth, and to wipe out the prejudices and superstitions of the days of ignorance. It cannot explain how a man could emerge from this environment who looked beyond the watertight compartments of race, nation, and culture. It cannot tell us how this environment gave rise to a man who laid the foundations of a moral, spiritual, and cultural superstructure for the good of the world and not for his country alone. A man who practically, not theoretically, placed business transactions, politics, and international relations on moral grounds and produced such a balanced synthesis between worldly and spiritual life that even to this day, it is considered a masterpiece of wisdom and foresight. Can anyone honestly call such a person the product of the impenetrable darkness which saturated Arabia?

Not only does he appear to be independent of his environment. Rather, when we look at his achievements we are irresistibly drawn to the conclusion that he breaks through all temporary and physical barriers and passes beyond centuries and millenniums. Within his example is comprehended all human activity throughout the entire history of mankind.

He is not one of those whom history has cast into oblivion. He is not praised only because he was a good leader in his own time. He is that unique and incomparable leader of humanity who marches with time, who is modern in every age, just as he was in his own era of history. Truly his teachings are as modern as tomorrow's morn.

Those whom people call 'makers of history' are only 'creatures of history'. In fact, in the whole history of mankind, he is the unique example of a 'maker of history'. One can scan the lives of great leaders of the world who brought about revolutions and one will find that, on each occasion, the forces of revolution are gathering momentum for the destined upheaval. The forces were moving in certain directions and were only waiting for a favorable moment to burst forth. By harnessing these forces in time for action, the revolutionary leader played the part of an actor for whom the stage is already set. On the contrary, amidst all 'makers of history' and revolutionary figures of all times, he is the only person who had to find ways and means to bring about the requirements of revolution. He alone had to mold and produce the kind of men he wanted for his purpose because the spirit of revolution and its necessary furnishings did not exist in the people among whom he lived.

By his forceful personality, he made a permanent impression on the hearts of thousands of his disciples and molded them according to his liking. By his iron will he prepared the ground for revolution, molded its shape and features, and directed the current of events into a channel as he desired. Can anyone cite another example of a maker of history of such distinction, another revolutionary of such brilliance and splendor?

The Final Testimony

One may ponder over this matter and wonder how, in the dark ages 1400 years ago and in a backward region like Arabia, an illiterate Arab trader and herdsman came to possess such light, such knowledge, such power, such talents, and such fine moral virtues?

One could say there is nothing peculiar about his message. It is the product of his own mind. If it is so, then he should have proclaimed himself to be God. If he had made such an assertion, the peoples of the earth who did not hesitate to call Krishna and Buddha gods and Jesus the Son of God, and who could, without the least bit of guilt, worship even the forces of nature — would have readily acknowledged this wonderful person as the Lord God Himself.

But lo! His assertion is just to the contrary. For he proclaimed that: "I am a human being like yourselves. I have not brought anything to you of my own accord. It has all been revealed to me by God. Whatever I possess belongs to Him. This message the like of which the whole humanity is unable to produce, is the message of God. It is not the product of my mind. Every word of it has been sent down by Him, and glory be to Him Whose message it is. All the wonderful achievements which stand to my credit in your eyes, all the laws I have given, all the principles I have spoken of—none of them is from me. I find myself totally incompetent for producing such things. I look to Divine guidance in all matters. Whatever He wills I do, what He directs I proclaim."

What a wonderful and inspiring example of truth, honesty, honor, and integrity it is! A liar and a hypocrite tries to ascribe to himself all the credit for the works of others, even when the falsehood of his claim can easily be proved. But this great man does not assign the credit for any of these achievements to Himself. He assigns absolutely no credit to himself even when none could contradict him, as there was no way of finding out the source of his inspiration.

56

What more proof of honesty of purpose, sincerity of character, and sublimity of soul can there be? Who else can be more truthful than he who received such unique gifts through a secret channel and still outrightly points out the source of his inspiration? All this leads us to the irresistable conclusion that this man was the true messenger of God.

Such was our prophet Muhammad (peace be on him). He was a man of extraordinary merits, a perfect example of purity and goodness, and a symbol of truth and justice. He was a great apostle of God, His messenger to the entire world. His life and thought, his truth and honesty, the goodness of his character, his system of thought and his achievements—all stand as undeniable proofs of his prophethood. Anyone who studies his life and teachings without bias will testify that without doubt, he was the true prophet of God and the Qur'an—the book he gave to mankind—is the true book of God. No unbiased and serious seeker of truth can escape this conclusion.

It must also be clearly understood that through Muhammad alone can we know the straight path of Islam. The Qur'an and the example of Muhammad are the only reliable sources available for mankind to learn God's Will in its totality. Muhammad is the messenger of God for the whole human race and the long chain of prophets came to an end with him. He was the last prophet and all the instructions God wished to give mankind through direct revelation were sent by Him through Muhammad. This revelation is enshrined in the Qur'an and the Sunnah.[1] Whoever be a seeker of truth and is anxious to become an honest Muslim, a sincere follower of the way of God, it is mandatory for him to believe in God's last prophet. He must accept his teachings and follow the way he pointed out to man. This is the real road to success and salvation.

---

[1] The Sunnah is the preserved teachings, sayings and life-example of Muhammad.

IV

THE FINALITY OF PROPHETHOOD

This brings us to the question of the finality of prophethood. Let's now consider this in relation to the prophethood of Muhammad (peace be on him).

We already discussed the nature of prophethood and this discussion makes it clear that the advent of a prophet is not an everyday event. Nor is the presence *in person* of the prophet essential for every land, people, or period. The life and teachings of the prophet are the beacon-light to guide people to the Right Path. As long as his teachings and guidance are alive, he is, as it were, himself alive. The real death of a prophet consists not in his physical demise but in the neglect of his teachings and the interpolation of his guidance. Earlier prophets have died only because their followers adulterated their teachings, altered their instructions, and defiled their life-examples by attaching false stories to them. Not one of the earlier books —the Torah of Moses, the Psalms of David, the Gospel of Jesus, etc.—exists today in its original form. Even the followers of these books confess they do not possess the *original* books. The biographies of the earlier prophets are so mixed up with fiction that an accurate and authentic account of their lives has become impossible. Their lives have become tales and legends and no trustworthy record is available anywhere. It cannot even be said with certainty when and where a given prophet was born, where and how he lived, and what law he gave to mankind. The fact is, the real death of a prophet lies in the death of his teachings.

Judging the facts on this standard, no one can deny that Muhammad and his teachings are alive. His teachings stand uncorrupted and are incorruptable. The Qur'an— the book he gave to mankind—exists in its original form, without the slightest alteration of letter, syllable, or word. The entire account of his life—his sayings, instructions, and actions—is preserved with complete accuracy. So great is this truth that even after the lapse of fourteen centuries its illustration in history is so clear and complete that it seems as if we are seeing him with the eyes under our brow. The biography of no other human being is so well preserved as that of Muhammad (peace be on him). Even the exact date and place of his birth is known with certainty. In every aspect of life we can seek guidance from Muhammad and learn a lesson from his example. This is why there is no need for any other prophet after Muhammad, the last of the prophets (peace be on him).

Furthermore, there are three things which require the advent of a new prophet: just the replacement of a departed prophet is not a good enough reason. These things can be summed up as follows:

1. That the teachings of all earlier prophets have been changed, corrupted or lost and their revival is needed. In this case, a new prophet is raised so he can purge the impurities from the people's lives and restore the system of God to its original form, or

2. That the teachings of a prophet who has died were incomplete and it is necessary to amend them, improve on them, or add to them. So a new prophet is sent to bring about these improvements, or

3. That the earlier prophet was raised specifically for a certain nation or territory and a prophet for another nation, people, or country would be required.

These are the three fundamental conditions which require that a new prophet be raised up. A careful review of the facts shows that none of these conditions exists today. The teachings of the last prophet, Muhammad (peace be on him) are alive, have been fully preserved, and are made immortal. The guidance he showed mankind is complete and flawless, guidance which is enshrined in the Qur'an. As for the Qur'an, there is nothing more authentic in all human history than this fact about it: it is the same Qur'an to the exact letter as the one revealed to Muhammad over 1400 years ago. All other sources of Islam are fully intact. This is so much the case that each instruction, every action of the prophet can be ascertained without the least shadow of a doubt. Thus, since his teachings are totally intact, there is no need for any new prophet to appear. The role of a prophet is accomplished by his example: what he says and does, how he acts and lives. If these teachings and actions are kept historically alive, it is as if he himself remains alive.

Secondly, God Almighty has completed His revealed guidance through prophet Muhammad for mankind. God Most Great says: "Today I have perfected your religion for you and completed my bounty on you," and a thorough study of Islam as a complete system of life proves the truth of these Qur'anic words. Islam gives guidance for life in this world as well as how to prepare for our journey to the hereafter; nothing essential for man's guidance has been left out. This system of life has now been perfected and there is no ground for new prophethood on the plea of imperfection.

Lastly, the message of Muhammad (peace be on him) was not meant for any particular people, place, or period. He was sent as the World Prophet—the messenger of truth for the entire mankind. The Qur'an commanded Muhammad to declare: "O mankind I am God's messenger to all of you." The Qur'an calls him "a blessing for all the people of the worlds." Without doubt, his approach was universal and humanitarian. This is why after him, there is no need for new prophethood and the Qur'an describes Muhammad as the last of the chain of true prophets.

Because of this, the only source for anyone to know about God and His system of life is Muhammad (peace be on him). We can understand Islam only through his teachings, which are so comprehensive that they can guide men for all times to come. The world does not now need another new prophet. It only needs men who put all their faith in Muhammad, who become the standard-bearers of his message, who propagate it to the world, and seek to establish the culture which Muhammad gave to man. The world needs men of good character who can translate his teachings into practice in order to establish a society governed by Divine law. It needs those men who work to establish the society, God's society, whose supremacy Muhammad came to establish. This is the mission of Muhammad and on its success hinges the success of man.

CHAPTER FOUR

THE ARTICLES OF FAITH

Before we proceed further, the earlier discussions should be reviewed. We can summarize them as follows:

1. Islam stands for complete submission and obedience to God, the Lord of the Universe. The only authentic source of knowing about Him, His Will, and His Law is the teachings of the true prophet. So we can define Islam as that religion which calls for complete faith in the prophet's teachings. It stands for complete obedience to the system of life shown to us by the prophet. Consequently, any who ignores the medium of the prophet and claims to follow God directly is not a Muslim.

2. In earlier ages, separate prophets appeared in different nations. The history of prophethood shows that several prophets often appeared in the same nation, one after the other. Then too, Islam was the name of the religion which these men taught. Though the basic principles of Islam were the same in every age and in each country, minor differences existed. These minor differences occurred in the methods of worship, codes of law, and in other detailed rules as needed to suit the conditions of each particular locale and people. This made it totally unnecessary for any given nation to follow the prophet of another land and people. The responsibility of each people was only to follow the instructions of their own prophet.

3. This period of many prophets ended with the advent of Muhammad (peace be on him). The teachings of Islam were made complete through him. One basic law was formed for the whole world and he was made a prophet for the entire mankind. His prophethood was not meant for any particular nation, country, or period. His message is for all peoples and for all times. The earlier prophetic

codes were abrogated by the advent of Muhammad, who gave the world a complete system of life. Now there will be no prophet appearing in the future, nor will any new religious system be revealed. The fact is Muhammad's teachings are meant for all the children of Adam, are sent for the entire human race, and are valid until the end of time. Since to follow Muhammad is what Islam is all about, one must: recognize his prophethood, believe in everything he has asked us to believe in, follow him in letter and spirit, and submit to all his commands and rules as the commands and rules of Almighty God. This is Islam.

This raises the question: What has Muhammad asked us to believe in? What are the articles of Islamic faith? We shall try to discuss these articles and see how simple, how true, how lovable, and how valuable they are. We shall try to see to what great height they raise the status of man both in this world and in the life to come!

I

BELIEF IN THE ONENESS OF GOD

The most basic and important teaching of prophet Muhammad (peace be on him) is belief in the Oneness of God. This is expressed in the primary statement of Islam that "There is no other god but God." This beautiful phrase is the bedrock of Islam. It is its foundation and is the essential prerequisite for being a Muslim. It is this expression which differentiates a true Muslim from an unbeliever; one who associates others with God in His Authority, or an atheist. The acceptance or denial of this phrase produces a world of difference between men. Those who believe in it become a single community and those who do not believe in it form the opposite group. For the believers there is progress which cannot be restricted. There is success whose heights cannot be measured. There is unlimited success both in this life and in the hereafter, while failure and humiliation are results met by those who refuse to believe in it.

But the difference which occurs between the believers and unbelievers is not the result of mere chanting of a few words. The real force lies in the conscious acceptance of this doctrine and the demands it makes upon us. Its real power lies in following it completely in everyday life. Unless you know the meaning of "There is no other god but the one Great and Almighty God", and the significance its acceptance has on human life, you cannot realize how important it truly is. This statement will never become effective unless its meaning and significance is clearly understood. Just by repeating the word "food" we cannot dull the edge of hunger; mere chanting of a medical prescription cannot heal the disease. In the same way, if the meaning behind the concept of the Oneness of God is fully grasped, it will help us avoid, in belief as well as action, every shade of disbelief, atheism, and polytheism. This is the natural result of believing in the Oneness of God.

The Meaning of this Statement

In the Arabic language, the word *ilah* means 'one who is worshipped', i.e. a being which because of its greatness and power is considered worthy to be worshipped, to be bowed to in humility and submission. Anything possessing power too great to be comprehended by man is also called *ilah*. The concept of ilah also includes that it possesses infinite powers; powers which may astonish others. It means that others are dependent upon ilah and that ilah is not dependent upon anyone else. This word also carries a sense of concealment and mystery; that is, ilah would be a being unseen and imperceptible. The word *khuda* in Persian, *deva* in Hindi, and *god* in English bear the same significance. Other languages also contain words with a like sense.

The word *Allah*, on the other hand, is the essential personal name of God. *La ilaha illallah* literally means "There is no *ilah* other than the One Great Being known by the name *Allah*." It means that in the whole universe, there is absolutely no being worthy to be worshipped other than Allah. It means that it is only to Him that heads should bow in adoration. It means that He is the only Being Who possesses all the powers, that all are in need of His favor, and that all must seek His help. He is concealed from our senses, and our intelligence fails to perceive what He is.

Having understood the meaning of these words, let's now find out their real significance.

If we go back to the most ancient eras of human history, or if we investigate the oldest relics of antiquity, we find that in every age man recognized a god or group of gods. Man not only recognized them but also worshipped them. Even today every nation on earth from the most primitive to the most civilized, believes in and worships some kind of god. This shows that the idea of having a god and paying tribute to him is ingrained in human nature. There is something within man's soul which forces him to this realization.

But the question now is: What is that thing and why does man feel compelled to act this way? The answer can be discovered if we look into the position of man in this huge universe. A study of man and his nature shows that he is not all-powerful, all-knowing, and all-seeing. Neither is he self-sufficient and self-existing. Nor are his powers unlimited. In fact, he is weak, frail, needy, and destitute. He is dependent upon a number of forces and without their assistance he cannot make headway. There are countless things which are needed to maintain his existence, but all of them are not totally within his grasp. Sometimes he gets hold of them in a simple and natural way. At other times, he finds himself deprived of them. There are many important and valuable items which he wants to get, but sometimes he succeeds in getting them and at other times he fails. It is not completely within his power to obtain them. Many things hinder his attempts; accidents destroy all his life-long work in a single moment. Taking chances can bring his hopes to a sudden end. Disease, worries, and calamities always threaten him and mar his way to happiness. He may try to get rid of these problems—but both success and failure may hit him at the same time.

The greatness and grandeur of many things overawe him: mountains and rivers, gigantic animals and ferocious beasts. He experiences earthquakes, storms, and other natural disasters. He observes clouds over his head and sees them becoming thick and dark. Then, he sees bolts of lightning, hears blasts of thunder, and is overwhelmed by the torrential fall of rain which comes forth from them. He sees the sun, the moon and the stars in their constant motion. He reflects as to how great, powerful, and majestic these bodies are, and in contrast how frail and insignificant he himself is! The vast wonders of the universe, on the one hand, and the consciousness of his own frailty, on the other, impress him with a deep sense of his weakness. He realizes how humble and helpless he really is. And it is quite natural that his initial ideas about divine beings coincides with this sense. He thinks of the hands which are wielding these great forces. The sense of their greatness makes him bow in humility. The sense of their power makes him seek their help. He tries to please them so they will be kind and helpful to him; and he dreads them and tries to escape their wrath so he will not be destroyed by them.

In the most primitive stage of ignorance, man thinks that the objects of nature whose greatness is easily visible and which appear to be helpful or harmful to him, hold in themselves the real power and authority. Therefore, he assumes them to be divine. Thus, he worships trees, animals, rivers, mountains, fire, rain, air, heavenly bodies, and numerous other objects. This is the worst form of ignorance.

When his ignorance dissipates somewhat, and a glimmer of light and knowledge is shed on his mind, he realizes that these great and powerful objects are themselves quite helpless and are in no way better situated than man. Rather, they are more dependent and helpless still. The largest and strongest animal dies like a tiny germ and loses all its power. Great rivers rise and fall and become dry. The high mountains are blasted and shattered by man himself. The earth's productivity is not under its own control—water makes it prosperous and lack of water makes it barren. Even water is not independent. It depends on air currents and the atmosphere which forms the clouds. Air too is powerless, and its usefulness rests on other forces. The moon, the sun, and the stars are also bound up by a powerful law outside whose mandates they cannot make even the slightest movement. After realizing this, man's mind turns to the possibility that some great, mysterious power of divine nature exists — some power which controls the objects he sees. It must be a power which is the source of all authority. His reflections then give rise to belief in mysterious powers, powers which are behind the natural phenomena. Innumerable gods are thought to be governing the various aspects of nature such as air, light, water, etc. Suggestive forms or symbols are constructed to represent them. This too is a form of ignorance, and reality still remains hidden from the eye.

As man progresses further in knowledge, and as he reflects more deeply about life, he finds that the universe is controlled by an all-powerful law which governs all that exists. What complete regularity is observed in the sunrise and sunset, in the winds and rain, in the motions of stars and changes of seasons. How in such a wonderfully harmonious way countless different forces are working together. What a highly potent and supremely wise law it is, according to which all the things in the universe are made to work—and how unbelievably intelligent a law it is that these forces work together to produce a given event at a specific time. And this without error, disarray, and confusion! Observing this uniformity, this regularity, and this complete obedience to a firm law in all fields of nature, even a man who believes in many gods finds himself obligated to believe that there must be a deity greater than all others, who exercises supreme authority. For if there were separate, independent gods, the whole machinery of the universe would be upset.

Man calls this greatest God, this Supreme Authority, by different names. Some call him 'God', others call him 'Allah', 'Khuda', Dios', etc. But as the darkness of ignorance persists, man continues worshipping minor gods along with the Supreme One. He imagines that the Divine Kingdom of God is not different from earthly kingdoms. Just as a ruler has many ministers, governors, and other responsible officers, so the minor gods are like so many responsible officers under the Great God Who cannot be approached without pleasing and pacifying the officers under Him. So they must also be worshipped and appealed to and in no case should be offended. Thus they are regarded as agents through whom an approach can be made to the Great God.

The more man increases in knowledge, the more dissatisfied he becomes with the theory that there are a number of gods. So the number of minor gods begins to decrease. More enlightened men bring each of these gods under the searchlight of scrutiny and ultimately find that none of these man-made gods has any divine character. They themselves are creatures like man, rather more helpless. They are thus dropped out one by one until only one God remains. But the concept of one God still contains some remnants of the elements of ignorance. Some people imagine that He has a body like a human being and is living in a particular place. Some believe that God came to the earth in human form; others think that God, after settling the affairs of the universe, has retired and is now taking rest. Others believe it is necessary to approach God through the media of saints and spirits, and that nothing can be achieved without their intercession. Some imagine God to have a certain form or image, and they think it is necessary to keep that image before them for purposes of worship. Such distorted notions about God have persisted —many of them being prevalent among different people of even our present age.

The *Oneness of God* is the highest concept of godhead, the knowledge of which God sent to mankind in all ages through His prophets. It was his knowledge with which, in the beginning, Adam was sent down to the earth. It was the same knowledge that had been revealed to Noah, Abraham, Moses, and Jesus (God's blessings be on them all). It is *The* Knowledge, pure and absolute, without the least shade of doubt or falsehood. Man became guilty of associating others with God, idol worship, and disbelief only because he turned away from the teachings of the prophets. By turning away, he depended on his own faulty reasoning and on his inadequate ability to interpret the true facts of life. The concept of God's Oneness dispels all clouds of ignorance and brightens the horizon with the light of reality. Let's see what beautiful truths this concept of the *Oneness of God* conveys and what belief it fosters. To do this, we must consider the following two points:

First we are faced with the question of who or what is the real force in control of this world. We are face to face with a grand, majestic universe which has no limits, whose boundaries cannot be seen, the extent of whose dominion is only perceived by Almighty God. Man's mind, with its limited abilities, fails to discern its beginning and cannot visualize its end. It is moving on its chartered course from time immemorial and will continue its journey into the future. Creatures beyond number have appeared in it— and go on appearing every day. The phenomena are so bewildering that a thinking mind finds itself aghast and wonderstruck. Man is unable to understand how that great thing began—he cannot grasp the reality by his unaided vision. He cannot believe that all this appeared just by chance, that it occurred by accident. The universe is obviously not a mass of matter which has evolved into its present state just by chance. It is not a jumble of uncoordinated objects. It is not a conglomeration of things chaotic and meaningless. All this cannot be without a Creator, a Designer, Controller and a Governor. But who can create and control this majestic universe? Only He can do so Who is the Master of all, Who is infinite and eternal, Who is all-powerful and all-wise. Only He can control it Who hears and knows all things. He must possess limitless powers, must be the Lord of the universe and all that it contains. He must be free from every flaw and weakness and none can have the power to interfere with His work. Only such a Being can be the Creator, the Controller, and the Master of the universe.

Secondly, it is essential that all these divine characteristics rest in One Being—it is virtually impossible for two or more individuals having the same powers and qualities to co-exist. They are bound to collide. Therefore, there must be one and only one Supreme Being Who has control over all things. You cannot think of two governors for the same state or two supreme commanders for the same army! The distribution of these powers among different gods, for instance, that one is all-knowing, another all-governing, and still another life-giver—each having his own independent field of activity—is also unthinkable. The universe is an indivisible unit. In the above case, every one of these gods must be dependent on others to execute his specific task. Lack of coordination is bound to occur. And if this happens, the world is destined to go to pieces.

These godly qualities are also not transferable. It is not possible for a certain attribute to be present in a certain god at one time and at another time it is found in another god. A divine being who is incapable of remaining alive himself cannot give life to others. One who cannot protect his own divine power is definitely unsuited to govern the vast, limitless universe. Thus the more you reflect upon the problem, the firmer will be your conviction that all these divine qualities must exist in one Being alone. From this we can easily see that the worshipping of many gods is a form of ignorance and cannot stand rational scrutiny. It is a practical impossibility. The facts of life do not fit into the explanation. They automatically bring man to Reality, i.e. the *Oneness of God.*

Keeping in mind this correct and perfect conception of God, cast a searching glance at this huge universe. Exert yourself to the utmost and see if you find among all the objects you see, among all the things that you perceive, among all you can think, feel, or imagine—all that your knowledge can comprehend — anyone possessing these qualities. The sun, the moon, the stars, animals, birds, or matter, money, any man or group of men — does any of them possess these qualities? Does any one of them possess even a single attribute of God Almighty? Does any of them have even the slightest shred of any one of His qualities? Certainly none. Certainly none because everything in the universe is created, is controlled and is regulated. All things are dependent on other things, all are mortal and all exist for only a limited period of time. None of them are self-acting or self-propelled. Their slightest movements are controlled by an inflexible law and they cannot deviate from that law. The helpless condition of these things proves that the attire of godliness cannot fit their body. They do not possess the slightest trace of divinity and have absolutely nothing to do with it. Simply put, they are without godly powers and it is a travesty of truth and nonsense to the highest degree to raise them to divine status. This is what is meant by 'there is no other god but God' or 'no other creature, human, or material object possesses godly powers or authority deserving worship and obedience'.

But this is not the end of our search. We saw that no human or material elements in this universe have even the slightest trace of godly powers. This forces us to conclude that there is a Supreme Being, over and above all that our unwary eyes see in the universe. It is a Being Who is the Will behind all things, the Creator of this grand universe, the Controller of its magnificent Law, the Governor of its serene rhythm, the Administrator of all its workings—He is God, the Master of the Universe. There is no one associated with Him in His Divinity.

This profound knowledge is far superior to all other kinds of knowledge. The greater you look into this fact, the deeper will be your conviction that this is the starting point of all knowledge. In every field of study, whether it be physics, chemistry, astronomy, geology, biology, economics, politics, sociology, humanities, or any other, you will find that the deeper you probe into them, the clearer become the indications of the truth of 'there is no other god but God'. It is this concept which opens the doors of inquiry and investigation and brightens the pathways of knowledge with the light of truth. And if you deny or disregard this great truth, you will meet with disillusionment at every step you take. For denial of this primary truth robs everything in the universe of its real meaning and significance. The universe at large becomes meaningless and the visions of progress get blurred and confused forever.

The Effects of the Oneness of God on Human Life

Now let us study the effects which belief in 'there is no other god but Almighty God' has on the life of man. Let's see why one who accepts it will always be a success in life and one who rejects it becomes a failure, both here and in the hereafter.

1. A person who believes in this concept can never have a narrow-minded or degenerate outlook. He believes in a God Who is the Creator of the heavens and the earth. He worships that God Who is the Master of the East and the West, and Who is the Sustainer of the entire universe. After having this belief, he does not regard anything in this world as a stranger to himself. To him, everything belongs to the same Lord Whom he himself belongs to. He is not prejudiced in his thinking and behavior. His sympathy, love, and service do not remain confined to a particular sphere or group. His vision is enlarged, his intellectual horizon widened and his outlook becomes as liberal and as boundless as is the Kingdom of God. How can this width of vision and breadth of mind be achieved by an atheist, a polytheist, or one who believes in a god supposed to possess limited and defective powers (like a man)?

2. This belief produces within man the highest degree of self respect and self esteem. The believer knows that God Almighty alone is the possessor of all power. None besides Him can help or harm a person. He knows that no one but He can provide for his needs, can give and take away life, or wield authority or influence. This conviction makes him indifferent to, and independent and fearless of all powers other than those of God. He never bows his head in homage to any of God's creatures nor does he stretch his hand before anyone else. He is not overawed by anyone's greatness. These mental qualities cannot be produced by any other

belief. For it is necessary that those who associate other beings with God, or who deny the existence of God, should bow in homage to some lower creatures. And it is these creatures who they regard as able to help or hurt them, who they would fear, and in whom they would put all their hopes.

3. Along with self respect, this belief builds in man a sense of modesty and humbleness. It makes him seek neither show nor glory and he presents no false image. The boisterous pride of power, wealth, and worth have no room in his heart. They have no room for he knows that whatever he owns has been given to him by God and that God can take away just as He can give. In contrast, an unbeliever, when he achieves some worldly merit, becomes proud and conceited because he believes that his achievement is due to his own worth. Pride and conceit are also a necessary outcome of associating others with God in His divinity, because a man who worships many gods believes he has a special relationship with those 'gods', one which does not exist between them and other people.

4. This belief makes man virtuous and upright. He becomes convinced that there is no other means of success and salvation except purity of soul and righteousness of behavior. He has perfect faith in the God Who is above and beyond all needs, and Who is absolutely just. He knows that none else has any hand or influence in the exercise of His godly powers. This belief creates in man the feeling that unless he lives rightly and acts justly, he cannot succeed. No influence or underhanded activity can save him from being ruined if he doesn't follow this way. Contrasting this is the life of disbelievers. They always live on false hopes. Some believe that God's son has atoned for their sins; others think they are God's favorites and will not be punished. Some believe that their saints will intercede with God on their behalf while still others make offerings to their gods and believe that by so bribing them, they have acquired license for all the foolishness and ill-deeds and can do whatever they like. Such false beliefs keep them entangled in the meshes of sin and evil, and

being dependent on their gods, they neglect to purify their souls and live pure and good lives. As for the atheists, they do not believe that there is any being who has power over them to whom they would be responsible. They feel they are responsible to no one for their good or bad actions. Thus they consider themselves totally independent to act in whatever way they like. Their own desires become their gods, and they live like slaves to them.

5. The believer does not become despondent and broken hearted under any circumstances. He has firm faith in God Who is the Master of all the treasures of the heavens and earth, Whose kindness and bounty have no limit and Whose powers are infinite. This faith gives his heart extraordinary consolation. It fills it with satisfaction and keeps it filled with hope. This man might meet with rejection from all doors. Nothing in this life might serve his purposes. All means might, one after the other, desert him. But Faith in and dependence on God never leave him. Upon their strength he goes on struggling. Such profound confidence can result from no other belief than belief in one God. Unbelievers, atheists, and those who worship many gods have small hearts. Therefore in times of trouble, they are soon overwhelmed by despair and frequently commit suicide.

6. This belief produces in man a strong degree of determination. A man with this belief works for and trusts in God. One committed to it, he can devote his energies to fulfil the Divine Commands, thereby gaining the pleasure of God. And he knows he has the support and backing of the Lord of the universe in this effort. This certainty makes him firm and strong like a mountain and no amount of difficulties, roadblocks, and hostile opposition can make him give up his commitment. Association, unbelief, and atheism have no such effect.

7. This declaration inspires bravery in man. There are two things which make a man cowardly: (1) fear of death and a love for safety, and (2) the idea that there is someone else besides God who can take away life and that man, by adopting certain strategies, can ward off death. Belief

in 'there is no other god but Almighty God' purges the mind of both these ideas. The first concept is cleansed from his mind because he knows that his life, property, and everything else really belongs to God. Everything must return to Him so he doesn't mind sacrificing all of His pleasure. He rids himself of the second thought because he knows that no weapon, man, or animal has the power of taking away his life; God alone has the power to do so. A time of death has been ordained for him, and all the forces in the world combined cannot take away anyone's life a moment before the appointed time. It is for this reason that no one is braver than the man who has faith in God. Nothing can intimidate him. Even the tempests of adversity, the storms of opposition, and the mightiest armies cannot overcome him. When he comes out to fight for God, he overpowers a force even ten times greater than his own. When can the associators, the unbelievers, and the atheists obtain such great determination, force or power? They hold life to be the dearest of all in the world, and believe death is caused by the enemy and can be avoided by running away from him!

8. Belief in One God creates an attitude of peace and contentment. It purges the mind of the passions of jealousy, envy, and greed. It prevents man from using cruel and unjust means for achieving success. The believer knows that wealth is in God's hands, and that He passes it out more or less as He likes. He knows that honor, power, reputation, and authority—everything—is subjected to God's Will, and He bestows these things as He wishes. The believer realizes that man's duty is only to work and struggle fairly and that success and failure ultimately depend on God's grace. If He wills to give, no power can stop Him and if He does not want to, no power can force Him to give. On the other hand, the disbelievers and atheists consider success and failure as dependent upon their efforts alone and upon the help or opposition they find in earthly forces. They remain slaves to greed and envy. In achieving success, they never hesitate to use bribery, conspiracy, tyranny, and other kinds of oppressive means. Jealousy and envy of others' success eats them away, and they leave

no stone unturned in resorting to the worst possible measures to bring about the downfall of their successful rival.

9. The most important effect of belief in One God is that it makes man obey and observe God's Law. One who believes in it is certain that God knows everything that is hidden or in the open. He is sure that God is close to him, closer to him than his own jugular vein. If he commits a sin in a secluded area in the darkness of the night, God knows about it. Almighty God even knows our unexpressed thoughts and intentions, whether they are good or bad. We can hide from everyone, but we cannot hide from God. We can evade everyone but we cannot evade God's grip. The firmer a man believes in this, the more he will observe God's rules and regulations. He will shun what his Master has forbidden and will carry out His bequests even when he is by himself or when no one can see him. This is so because he knows God's 'police' never leave his presence, and he dreads the court whose warrant he can never avoid. It is for this reason that the first and most important condition for being a Muslim is to believe in no god but the One True God (la ilaha illallah). 'Muslim', as you have already been told, means one who is 'obedient to God'. It means one who is at peace with God. Being at peace with God, and being obedient to Him is impossible unless one firmly believes that there is none worthy to be worshipped but Almighty God. In the teachings of Muhammad (God's blessings be on him), belief in One God is the most important principle. It is the bedrock of Islam and the mainspring of its power. All other Islamic beliefs, commands, and laws stand firm on this foundation. All of them receive strength for this source. Take it away, and there is nothing left of Islam.

II

BELIEF IN GOD'S ANGELS

Prophet Muhammad (peace be on him) has further instructed us to believe in the existence of God's angels. This is the second article of Islam and is very important, because it absolves the concept of God's Oneness from all possible impurities. It makes this concept pure, simple, and free from the danger of every conceivable shade of polytheism.

The polytheists have associated two kinds of creatures with God:

a) Those which have material existence and can be seen with our eyes such as the sun, moon, stars, fire, water, animals, great men, etc.

b) Those who have no material existence and cannot be seen—the unseen beings who are believed to be engaged in the administration of the universe. For instance, one controls the air, another imparts light, another brings rain, and so on.

The alleged gods of the first type exist in this material world before man's eyes. The falsehood of their claim has been fully exposed by the statement 'there is no other god but Almighty God'. This is sufficient to dispose of the idea that they have any share in divinity or deserve any reverence whatsoever. The second kind, being immaterial, are hidden from the human eye and are mysterious; the polytheists are more inclined to put their faith in them. They consider them to be gods or God's Children. They make images of them and present offerings to them. In order to purify belief in the Oneness of God, and to clear it from admixture of the second type of 'god', this particular article of faith has been provided.

Muhammad (God's blessings be on him) has informed us that these spiritual beings which we cannot see, whom people believe to be gods or God's children, are really Almighty God's angels.

These angels have no share in His divinity. They are under His command and are so obedient that they cannot deviate from His commands by even the slightest fraction of an inch. God employs them to administer the affairs of His Kingdom, and they carry out His orders exactly and accurately. They have no authority to do anything on their own; they cannot present to God any plan conceived by themselves. They are not authorized even to intercede with God for any man. To worship them and to seek their help is degrading and debasing. For, on the first day of man's creation, God made them prostrate before Adam. He gave Adam greater knowledge than they possessed and passed them up in bestowing upon Adam the role of being God's representative on earth. What debasement can, therefore, be greater for man than prostrating before and seeking favor from those who prostrated before him!

Muhammad forbade us to worship angels and to associate them with God in His divinity. But he also informed us that they are the chosen creatures of God and are free from sin. God made them of a nature such that they are unable to disobey Him and they are ever engaged in carrying out His orders. He told us that these angels surround us on all sides, are attached to us, and are always in our company. They observe and record all our actions, good or bad. They preserve a complete record of every man's life. After death when we will be brought before God, they will present a full report of our life and works on earth, wherein we shall find everything correctly recorded. Not a single action will be left out, however insignificant or carefully concealed it may be.

We have not been informed of the intrinsic nature of the angels. Only some of their characteristics have been mentioned to us. The main point is that we have been asked to believe that they exist. We have no other means of knowing their nature or qualities. Therefore, it would be foolish for us to attribute any form or quality to them on our own accord. We must believe in them exactly as we have been asked to. To deny their existence is disbelief for first, we have no reason for such a denial and secondly, our denial of them would be tantamount to attributing untruth to Muhammad (God's blessings be on him). We believe in their existence only because God's true Messenger has informed us of it.

III

FAITH IN THE BOOKS OF GOD

The third article of Faith which Muhammad (God's blessing be on him) has commanded us to believe in is faith in the books of God, books which He sent to mankind through His Prophets before the time of Muhammad. These books were revealed in the same way that the Qur'an was revealed to Muhammad. We have been informed of the names of some of these books: the Books of Abraham, the Torah of Moses, Psalms of David, and the Gospel of Jesus Christ. We have not been informed of the names of books which were given to other prophets. Therefore with regard to other existing religious books, we are not in a position to say with certainty whether they originally were revealed books or not.

But we automatically believe that whatever books had been sent by God were all true.

Of these books, the Books of Abraham are extinct and not traceable in the existing literature. David's Psalms, the Torah, and the Gospel exist with the Jews and Christians. But the Qur'an tells us that people have changed, added to, and subtracted from the original texts of these books, and God's words have been mixed up with texts of their own making. This business of corruption and pollution of the books has been so extensive and so evident that even the Jews and Christians themselves admit they do not possess their original texts. Instead, they have only translations of the originals, and these in a language different than that which they were first presented in. They will admit that the current translations are actually translations of several previous works, wherein for centuries many alterations were made. And they will admit that even to this day changes are being made in the texts. Any unbiased Christian or Jewish historian will testify to this.

Upon studying these books, we find many passages and accounts which obviously cannot be from God. God's words and those of man are mixed together and we have no means of knowing what part is from God, and what part is from man. We have been commanded to believe in the earlier revealed books only in the sense to admit that, before the Qur'an, God also sent books through His Prophets. We are commanded to believe that these books were all from the same One God Who sent the Qur'an and that the sending of the Qur'an is not a new or strange event. It is a Book which only confirms, restates, and completes those divine instructions which people mutilated or lost in antiquity.

The Qur'an is the last of the divine books revealed by God and there are some important differences between it and the previous Books. These differences may be briefly stated as follows:

1. The original texts of former divine books were lost completely and only their translations exist today. The Qur'an, on the other hand, exists exactly as it had been revealed to the prophet. Not a word—not even a letter of it—has been changed. It is available in its original text and the Word of God has now been preserved for all times to come.

2. In the former divine books, man mixed his words with God's words, but in the Qur'an we find only the words of God—and in their pristine purity. This is admitted even by the opponents of Islam.

3. No other sacred book can be said on the basis of authentic, historical evidence to really belong to the same prophet to whom it is attributed. For some books, even in what age and to which prophet they were revealed is not known. As for the Qur'an, the evidence that it was revealed to Muhammad is so voluminous, so convincing, so strong, and so compelling that even the worst critic of Islam cannot cast doubt over it. This evidence is so vast and detailed that, concerning many verses and commandments of the Qur'an, even the occasion and place of their revelation is known with certainty. This is the conclusion forced upon us by an unbiased and critical analysis of history.

4. The former divine books were sent in languages which have been dead long ago. In the present era, no nation or community speaks these languages and there are only a few people who claim to understand them. Thus, even if

these books existed today in their original form, it would be virtually impossible for us to correctly understand them. Our inability to understand their contents would make it extremely difficult to put their commandments into practice. In fact, it is rare to find a scholar who understands even the basics of these languages, and our common man of today has literally no knowledge of them. The language of the Qur'an, on the other hand, is a living, vibrant language. Millions of people speak it, and millions more know and understand it. It is being taught in nearly every university of the world. Every man can learn it, and he who has no time to learn it can find men everywhere who know this language and can explain the meaning of the Qur'an.

5. All other existing sacred books found among different nations of the world have been addressed to a specific group of people. Every one of them contains a number of commands which are addressed to a particular period of history and which catered to the needs of that age only. They are neither needed today, nor can they now be properly put into practice. It is clear from this that these books were meant only for those particular people and none of them was meant for the whole world. They were not to be followed permanently even by the people to whom they were revealed. In contrast, the Qur'an has been addressed to all mankind. Not a single part of it can be suspected as having been addressed to a particular group of people. In the same manner, all the commands and rules in the Qur'an can be acted upon at every place and in every age. This fact proves that the Qur'an is meant for the whole world, and is the eternal code for human life.

6. No one can deny that the previous divine books also contain concepts of goodness and virtue. They also taught principles of morality and presented a way of life which was in harmony with God's pleasure. But none of them was comprehensive enough to embrace all that is needed for a good, clean human life, nothing lacking. Some of them excelled in one area, others in some other. It is the Qur'an and the Qur'an alone which enshrines not only all

that was good in the former books but also perfects the Way of God Almighty by presenting the complete system of life which comprehends all that is necessary for man on this earth.

7. Because of man's interference, many things have been inserted in these books which are against reality, revolting to reason, and contrary to every instinct of justice. There are things which are cruel and unjust and pollute man's thoughts and actions. Furthermore, things have been inserted which are obscene, indecent, and openly immoral. The Qur'an is free from such rubbish. It contains nothing which is against our reasoning and nothing in it can be proved wrong. None of its rules are unjust; nothing within it is misleading. Of indecency and immorality, not a trace can be found in it. From beginning to the end, the book is full of wisdom and truth. It contains the best of philosophy and the choicest of laws for human civilization. It points out the right road to follow, and guides man to success and salvation.

It is because of these special features of the Qur'an that all people of the world have been directed to believe in it. They have been told to give up all other books and follow it alone. This is because it contains all that is essential for living in harmony with God's pleasure. And after it, there remains absolutely no need for any other divine book.

The study of the difference between the Qur'an and other divine books makes it easy for us to understand that believing in the Qur'an and belief in other divine books is not the same.

Faith in the other divine books should be limited to the simple recognition that they were all from God, were true, and had been sent down to fulfill, in their time, the same purpose for which the Qur'an has been sent. On the other hand, belief in the Qur'an should be that *it is purely and absolutely God's words,* that *it is perfectly true,* that *every part of it is preserved,* that *everything mentioned in it is right,* that *it is the duty of man to carry out in each and every command of it,* and that *whatever is against it must be rejected.*

V

FAITH IN GOD'S PROPHETS

In the last chapter, we said that God's Messengers were raised among every people, and that they all brought essentially the same religion—Islam—which prophet Muhammad propagated. In this respect, all the Messengers of God stand on par with each other and belong in the same category. If a man rejects any one of them he, as it were, rejects them all. The reason is quite simple. Suppose ten men make the same statement. If you admit one of them to be true, you automatically commit yourself to accepting the remaining nine as true. If on the other hand, you reject one of them, by implication you reject them all. It is for this reason that, in Islam, it is necessary to have implicit faith in all the prophets of God. One who does not believe in any one of the prophets is an *unbeliever*, though he may profess faith in all others besides that particular one.

We are told in the traditions that the total number of prophets sent to different people at different times is 124,000. If you consider how long the earth has existed, and how many years it has been from the first human to our current age; if you consider the number of different peoples and societies that have passed through it, this number will not appear too great. We are required to believe in those prophets whose names have been specifically mentioned in the Qur'an. Regarding the rest, we are told that all prophets sent by God for the guidance of mankind are true. Thus, we believe in all the prophets raised in India, China, Iran, Egypt, Africa, Europe, and other countries of the world. But we are not in a position to be definite about a particular person outside the list of prophets named in the Qur'an. Whether or not he was a prophet is not left for us to decide, for we have not been told anything definite about him. Nor are we permitted to say anything bad against the holy men of other religions. It is quite possible that some of them were God's prophets, and their followers corrupted their teachings after their deaths, just as the followers of Moses and Jesus (God's peace be on them) have done. Therefore, whenever we express an opinion about them, it would be about the practices and rituals of their religions. As for the founders of those religions, we will be careful to remain silent lest we become guilty of irreverence towards a prophet.

There is no difference between these prophets and Muhammad in the sense that all were sent by God as His Messengers, and all were teaching the same straight path of 'Islam'. We have been ordered by the Qur'an to believe in them all alike. But in spite of their equality in this respect, there are the following three differences between Muhammad and other prophets:

1. The other prophets came to certain people for specific periods, while Muhammad has been sent for the whole world and for all times to come.

2. The teachings of these prophets have either completely disappeared from the world or whatever remains of them is not pure, and is found intermingled with many false and fictitious statements. For this reason, even if one wishes to follow their teachings he cannot do so. In contrast, the teachings of Muhammad (peace be on him), his biography, his lectures, his ways of living, his morals, habits, and virtues, in short, all the details of his life are preserved. Muhammad (peace be on him), therefore, is the only one of the whole line of prophets who is a living personality, and in whose footsteps it is possible to follow correctly and confidently.

3. The guidance imparted through the earlier prophets was not complete and did not cover all the necessary fields. Every prophet was followed by another who made alterations and additions in the teachings of his predecessors. In this way, the chain of reform continued. This is why the teachings of earlier prophets, after the lapse of a certain period of time, were lost in oblivion. Obviously, there was no need for preserving the earlier teachings when amended and improved guidance had taken their place. At last, the most perfect system of guidance was given to mankind through Muhammad and all previous codes were automatically abrogated. All others were abandoned because

it is both futile and foolish to follow an incomplete system while the complete one exists. He who follows Muhammad follows all the prophets, for whatever was good and workable in their teachings has been embodied in his teachings. Whoever rejects and refuses to follow Muhammad's teachings and chooses to follow some other prophet only deprives himself of the vast amount of useful and valuable instruction contained therein. He loses access to those profound teachings which never existed in the books of the earlier prophets and which were revealed only through the last of the prophets.

This is why it is now incumbent upon each and every person to have faith in Muhammad (peace be on him) and to follow him alone. To become a true Muslim (a follower of the prophet's way of life) a person must have complete faith in Muhammad and affirm that:

(a) He is a true prophet of God;

(b) His teachings are absolutely perfect, free from any defect or error;

(c) He is the last prophet of God. After him no prophet will appear till the day of judgment, nor is any other person going to appear in whom it would be essential for a Muslim to believe.

VI

BELIEF IN LIFE AFTER DEATH

The fifth article is belief in life after death. Prophet Muhammad (peace be on him) directed us to believe in resurrection after death and in the day of Judgment. The essential ingredients of this belief, as taught to us by him are as follows:

The life of this world and of all that is in it will come to an end on an appointed day. Everything will be annihilated. This day is called the day of reckoning, or the *last day*.

All the human beings who lived in the world since its inception will then be restored to life and will be presented before God Who will sit in court on that day. This is called 'Resurrection'.

The entire record of every man and woman—all of their good or evil deeds—will be presented before God for final judgment.

God shall finally determine the reward of every person. He will weigh everyone's good and bad deeds. One who excels in goodness will be rewarded; one whose evils and wrong acts outweigh his good deeds will be punished.

The reward and punishment will be administered justly. Those who emerge successful in this judgment will go to Paradise and the doors of eternal bliss will be opened to them. Those who are condemned and deserve punishment will be sent to Hell—the abode of fire and torture.

The Need of this Belief

Belief in life after death has always been a part of the teachings of the prophets. Every one of them asked their followers to believe in it. This has always been an essential condition of being a Muslim. All prophets declared that one who disbelieves or casts doubts upon it is an *unbeliever*. This is so, because denial of life after death makes all other beliefs meaningless. This denial also destroys the very sanction for a good life and man is driven to a life of ignorance and disbelief. A little reflection will make this clearer.

In your everyday life, whenever you are asked to do something, you immediately think: what is the benefit of doing it and what harm is involved in not doing it? This is the nature of man. He instinctively regards a useless action as totally unnecessary. You are never willing to waste your time and energy in useless and unproductive jobs. Nor are you eager to avoid a thing which is harmless. And the general rule is that the more you are convinced about the usefulness of a thing, the firmer would be your response to it. The more doubtful you are about its effectiveness, the more shaky and wavering would be your attitude. After all, why does a child put his hand in fire? —Because he doesn't know that fire burns. Why does a youth avoid studying?—Because he doesn't fully understand the benefits of education and doesn't believe what his elders try to impress on his mind.

Now think of the man who does not believe in the day of Judgment. Wouldn't he consider belief in God and a life in harmony with His system of no consequence? What value will he attach to a life in pursuit of His pleasure? To him neither obedience to God is of any advantage, nor disobedience to Him of any harm. How then would it be possible for him to faithfully follow the commandments of God, His prophet, and His book? What incentive would he have to undergo trials and sacrifices, what would give him the discipline to avoid excessive worldly pleasures? And if a man does not follow the Law of God and lives according to his own likes and dislikes, of what use is his belief in the existence of God, if any such belief he has?

This is not all. If you reflect still deeper, you will come to the conclusion that belief in life after death is the greatest determining factor in the life of a man. Its acceptance or rejection determines the entire course of his life and behavior.

The man who has in mind success or failure in this world alone will be concerned with the benefits and losses he will gain in this life only. He will not be willing to undertake any good act if he has no hope of gaining worldly interest. Nor will he try to avoid a wrong act if it is not injurious to his interests in this world.

But a man who believes in the next world as well and is convinced of the final consequences his acts will bring upon him, will look upon all worldly gains and losses as temporary. He would not stake his eternal reward for some temporary gain. He will look at things in their broader perspective, and will always keep the everlasting benefit or loss in view. This is the intelligent way of looking at this world. This man will do what is good, however costly it

86

be to him in terms of worldly gains, or however injurious it be to his immediate interest. No matter how charming a wrong act may appear, he will avoid it. Things will be judged by the viewpoint of their eternal consequences by him, and he will not submit to his whims or wishes.

Thus there is a radical difference between the beliefs, approaches, and lives of the two persons. One's idea of a good act is limited to what it can bring in this brief temporary life as a gain in money, property, and public recognition. For him, a good act is that by which he gains position, power, reputation, and worldly happiness. Such things become his objectives in life. Fulfillment of his wishes and self-glorification become the be-all and end-all of his life. And he never desists from using cruel and unjust means in their achievement. His conception of a wrong act is one which involves a risk or injury to his interests in this world, like loss of property and life, spoiling of health, loss of reputation, or some other unpleasant consequence. In contrast to this man, the believer's concept of good and evil would be quite different. To him, all that pleases God is good and all that invokes His displeasure and wrath is evil. A good act, according to him, will remain good even if he does not receive benefit from it in this world. He will perform what is right even if it means he must lose some worldly possession or injure his personal interests. For he is confident that God will reward him in the eternal life and that would be the real success. He will not fall prey to evil deeds merely for some worldly gain, for he knows that even if he escapes punishment in his short life on this planet, in the end he would be the loser and would not be able to escape punishment by the court of God.

So it is the belief or disbelief in life after death which makes man adopt different courses in life. It is absolutely impossible for a person who does not believe in the day of judgment to fashion his life as suggested by Islam. Islam says: "In the way of God, give *zakat* to the poor." His answer is "No, *zakat* will diminish my wealth. Instead, I will take interest on my money." And while collecting it, he wouldn't hesitate to soak up every bit of wealth or belongings which the people who owe him have, though they be poor or hunger-stricken. Islam says: "Always speak the truth and shun lying, though you may gain greatly by lying and lose a great deal by speaking the truth." But his reply would be: "What should I do with a truth which is of no use to me here, and which instead brings loss to me? Why should I avoid lying where it can benefit me without any risk, even that of giving me a bad reputation?" He visits a secluded area and finds a precious metal lying there; in such a situation Islam says: "This is not your property, do not take it". But he would say: "I came across this thing without any cost or trouble; why shouldn't I take it? No one is around who might see me pick it up, who might report it to the police. No one is here who could give evidence against me in court, or discredit my reputation in front of the people. Why shouldn't I make use of this treasure?" Someone secretly keeps a deposit with this man, and after he dies, Islam commands: "Be honest with the property deposited with you and hand it over to the heirs of the deceased." He says: "Why?—There is no evidence of this property being with me; his children also don't know I have it. When I can confiscate it without any difficulty, without fear of legal claims or stain on my reputation, why should I not do so?" In short, at every step in life, Islam will direct him to walk in a certain direction and adopt a certain attitude of behavior, but the unbeliever will steer himself in the opposite direction. This is so because Islam measures everything from the viewpoint of its everlasting consequence, while such a person always has only the immediate and earthly outcome in view. Now you can understand why a man cannot be a Muslim without belief in the Day of Judgment. To be a Muslim is a very great thing; the fact is one cannot even become a good man without this belief. For the denial of the Day of Judgment degrades man from the great height of being a thinking, human creature to a place even lower than the lowest of animals.

LIFE AFTER DEATH: A RATIONAL VINDICATION

So far we have discussed the need and importance of belief in the Day of Judgment. We must now consider how sensible and understandable the components of this belief really are. The fact is that whatever Muhammad (peace be on him) has told us about life after death can clearly be understood through reason. Although our belief in that Day is based upon our full trust in the Messenger of God, clear and unbiased thinking not only confirms this belief but also reveals that Muhammad's teachings about it are much more reasonable and understandable than all other viewpoints in this area.

In the world today, the following viewpoints concerning life after death are found:

1. Some people say that there is nothing left of man after death, and that after this life-ending event, there is no other life. According to these people, belief in life after death has no reality. They say that there is no possibility of it and such a belief is quite unscientific. This is the view of the atheists who also claim to be scientific in their approach, bringing forth Western science for support.

2. Another group claims that man, in order to bear the consequences of his deeds, is repeatedly regenerated in this world. If he lives a bad life, in the next generation he will assume the shape of an animal, like a dog or a cat, etc. He could be reborn into some form of vegetation, like a tree or shrub, or even as some 'lower' kind of man. If his acts have been good, he will be reborn as a man into a higher class. This viewpoint is found in some Eastern religions.

3. There is a third viewpoint which calls for belief in the Day of Judgment, the Resurrection, man's presence in the Divine Court, and the administration of reward and punishment. This is the common belief of all the Prophets.

Now let us consider each of these viewpoints one by one.

The first group, which arrogates to itself the authority and support of science, alleges that there is no reality in life after death. They say that they have never seen anybody come back after his death. There is not a single case of revival. We see that after death a man is reduced to dust. Therefore, death is the end of life and there is no life after death. But just think over this reasoning: is this really a scientific argument? Is the claim really founded on reason? If they have not seen a case of revival after death, they can only say *they do not know what will happen after death*. But, instead of remaining within this limit, they declare that *nothing will happen after death* at the same time claiming that they speak out of knowledge! In fact, they merely generalize on ignorance. Science tells us nothing—negative or positive—in this respect and their assertion that life after death has no existence is totally unfounded. Their claim is not any different from the claim of an ignoramus who has not seen an airplane and on that 'knowledge' proclaims that airplanes do not exist at all! If a person has not seen a thing, it does not mean that thing does not exist. We cannot see oxygen and other such gases; yet we know they exist. We cannot even see the atom; we can only speculate as to its true form. No man, not even the entire humanity, if it has not seen a thing, can claim that such a thing does not, or cannot, exist. This claim is illusionary and is out and out unscientific. No reasonable man can give it any weight.

Now look at the belief of the second group. According to them, a human being is a human being because in his previous animal form he performed good deeds. An animal is an animal because previously as a human being he behaved badly. In other words, to be a man or an animal is the consequence of one's deeds in one's former form. One might well ask: "Which of them existed first, man or animal?" If they say man preceded animal, then they will have to admit that he must have been an animal before that, and was given a human form for its good deeds. If they say it was animal they will have to concede that there must have been a man before who was transformed into an animal for his bad deeds. This puts us into a vicious cycle and the advocates of this belief cannot settle any form for the first creature—every new generation implies a preceding generation so that the succeeding generation may be considered as a consequence of the former. This is simply absurd.

90

Now consider the third viewpoint. Its first claim is "This world will one day come to an end. God, the All-Powerful, will destroy and annihilate the universe. He will, in its place, evolve another higher and far superior cosmos."

This statement is undeniably true. No doubt can be cast upon its truthfulness. The more we reflect upon the nature of the cosmos, the more clearly it is proved that the existing system is not permanent and everlasting. All the forces working in it are limited in their nature, and we can be sure that one day they will be completely exhausted. This is why the scientists agree that on one day, the sun will become cold and will lose all its energy. The stars will collide with one another, and the whole system of the universe will be upset and destroyed. And if evolution is true for certain parts of the universe, why would it not be true for the universe in its entirety? To think of the universe becoming totally non-existent is more improbable than that it will pass into another evolutionary stage and another order of existence will emerge in a much more improved and ideal order.

The second proposition of this belief is that "Man will again be given life." Is it impossible? If so, how did the present life of man become possible? It is obvious that God Who created man in this world can do so in the next. Not only is it a possibility, it is also a positive necessity, as will be shown later.

The third claim is that "The record of all the actions of man in this world is preserved and will be presented on the Day of Resurrection." The proof of the truth of this statement is provided today by science itself. It was first understood that the sounds which we make produce slight waves in the air and die out. Now it has been discovered that sound leaves its impression on surrounding objects and can be reproduced. Stereo records are made on the same principle. From this, it can be understood that the record of every movement of man is being impressed on all things which come into contact with the waves he produces by these movements. This shows that the record of all our deeds is completely preserved and can be reproduced.

The fourth proposition is "On the day of Resurrection,

God will hold His court and, with just judgment, reward or punish man for his good and bad deeds." What is unreasonable about it? Reason itself demands that God should hold His court and be just in judgment therein. We see here that a man does a good deed and gains nothing from it in this world. We see another man who does a bad deed and does not suffer for it here. Not only this, we see thousands of cases of a good act resulting in trouble for the doer and of a bad deed resulting in the happiness and satisfaction of the guilty person. When we see these events happening every day, our reason and sense of justice demand that a time must come when the man who does good must be rewarded and the one who does evil will be punished. The way things presently exist is that things are subject to physical law. It is quite natural that a man who has the means to do evil things will do so according to that physical law. And it is not necessary that the bad consequences of his evil action react upon him here wholly or in part. If you have a can of gas and some matches, you can set the house of your opponent on fire and escape every consequence of this action (if the forces of this world are in your favor). Does this mean that this offense has no consequence at all? Certainly not! It only means that its physical result has appeared, and the moral result is reserved. Do you really think it reasonable that it should never appear? If you say it should, the question is, where? Certainly not in this world, because in this physical world only physical consequences of actions manifest themselves fully, while logical and moral results do not come forth. Results of this higher category can appear only if there comes into existence another order of things wherein logical and moral laws reign supreme and occupy the governing position. In such a high order, the physical laws are actually made subject to the moral ones. This is the next world which is the next evolutionary stage of the universe. It is evolutionary in the sense that it will be governed by moral laws rather than physical ones. The rational consequences of man's actions, consequences which were not fully accounted for in this life, will appear therein. Man's status will be determined by how well he fared in the test of this worldly life, the good and moral worth he attained therein. There you will not see an upright man serving under a fool, or a morally superior man in a position inferior to a wretch, as is often true in this world.

The last proposition of this belief is the existence of Paradise and Hell, which is also not impossible. If God can make the sun, the moon, the stars, and the earth, why shouldn't He be able to make Heaven and Hell? When He holds His court, and pronounces His judgments, rewarding the meritorious and punishing the guilty, there must be a place where the condemned might feel debasement, pain, and misery. And there must be another place where the good might enjoy their reward — an endless source of honor, happiness, peace, and contentment.

After considering these questions, no reasonable person can escape the conclusion that belief in life after death is the most acceptable to reason. No one can deny that this belief is the one which makes most sense. No unbiased thinker can say that there is anything unreasonable or impossible about it. More importantly, when a true Prophet like Muhammad (peace be on him) has stated this to be a fact, and it involves nothing but what is good for us, wisdom lies in believing in it completely. We must not reject it without any sound reasons.

The above are the five articles of Faith which form the foundation for the superstructure of Islam. Their summary is contained in the short sentence known as *Kalima Tayyibah*. When you declare *la ilaha illallah* (there is no god other than God) you give up all false gods, and profess that you are a creature of the One God. And when you add the words *Muhammad-ur-Rasulullah* (Muhammad is God's Messenger) you confirm and admit the Prophethood of Muhammad. With the admission of his Prophethood, it becomes obligatory that you believe in the divine nature and attributes of God, His angels, His Revealed Books, and in the life after death. You must then earnestly follow that method of obeying God and worshipping Him which Prophet Muhammad asked us to follow. Herein lies the road to success and salvation.

CHAPTER FIVE

PRAYER AND WORSHIP

From the earlier discussion we know that prophet Muhammad (peace be on him) told us to believe in five articles of faith:

(1)   Belief in the Oneness of God.

(2)   Belief in God's angels.

(3)   Belief in God's books, and in the Qur'an as His last book.

(4)   Belief in God's prophets, and in Muhammad as His final Messenger.

(5)   Belief in life after death.

These five articles make up the bedrock of Islam. One who believes in them enters the fold of Islam and becomes a member of the Muslim community. But by mere verbal profession alone, one does not become a complete Muslim. To become a complete Muslim one must fully put into practice the instructions given by Muhammad (peace be on him) as ordained by God. This is because belief in God makes practical obedience to Him mandatory; and it is obedience to God which constitutes the religion of Islam. By this belief you profess that Allah, the one God, is alone your God. This means that He is your Creator and you are His creature. It means He is your Master and you are His servant; that He is your Ruler and you are His subject. After acknowledging Him as your Master and Ruler, if you refuse to obey Him you are a rebel on your own admission.

Along with belief in God, you believe that the Qur'an is God's book. This means you admitted all the contents of the Qur'an to be from God. Thus it becomes your duty to accept and obey whatever is contained in it. Besides this, you admitted Muhammad (peace be on him) to be

God's Messenger. By doing so, you admitted that every one of his orders is from God. After accepting this, being obedient to him becomes your duty. For there is no Islam without belief in and obedience to the Messenger of God. From this you can tell that you become a full-fledged Muslim only when you profess what the prophet professed and practice what the prophet practiced. And you must then practice what you preach. Otherwise, your Islam will remain incomplete.

Now let's see what rules Muhammad (peace be on him) taught, rules which were ordained by Almighty God. First and foremost of these are the acts of worship or the *primary duties which must be observed by every person professing to be a Muslim.*

ACTS OF WORSHIP

The Arabic word defining these arts of worship is *ibadat.* This is derived from the word 'abd' which means submission. 'Abd' also can be defined as something 'owned' by someone else. What all this really means is that God is your Master and you are His servant and whatever a servant does in obeying his Master, whatever he does for the pleasure of his Master, is an act of worship. This Islamic concept of worship is very wide. If you remove from your speech false, malicious, and abusive things, and speak the truth and talk about good and helpful things; if you do all this because God Almighty has told you to, this constitutes a form of worship. They are acts of worship no matter how secular their appearance might be. If you obey the law of God across the board in your commercial and economic affairs, if you use it in your dealings with your parents, relatives, and friends, clearly these activities become acts of worship. If you help the poor and handicapped, feed the hungry and serve the ailing, and if you do all this not for any personal gain, but to seek the pleasure of God, they are nothing short of acts of worship. Even your money earning activities—your jobs—the activities you undertake to earn your living and feed your dependents—are acts of worship if you remain honest in performing them and observe the law of God. In short, all your activities and your entire life are acts of worship if your heart is filled with fear and love of God while performing them. Your entire life is worship if your ultimate objective in life is to seek the pleasure of the Great and Wonderful God.

From this we can conclude that whenever you do good or avoid evil out of fear of God, no matter what aspect of life you might name, you are performing your Islamic obligations. This is the true meaning of the concept of worship in Islam. It is equal total submission of man to the pleasure of Almighty God. Total submission means we will mold our entire life into the patterns of Islam, such that even the most minor details of it won't be left out. To help achieve this objective, a set of formal acts of worship is prescribed to serve as a course in training. They equip individuals with the necessary tools so they can work for Almighty God. The more diligently we follow the training, the better equipped we will be for the task ahead. And this is a great task. For, by so training we will effectively bind together both what we practice and what we preach, thereby moving in the correct direction for which we were created. What could be greater than to move in the direction of God Almighty by performing what he has asked us to perform, by working in the way He has asked us to work? It is for this reason that the acts of worship are considered the pillars on which the foundation of Islam stands.

SALAT

Salat is the most important of these obligations. And what is *salat*? It is the prescribed daily prayers which consist of repeating and refreshing the belief you put your trust in. It is performed five times a day. You get up in the morning, cleanse yourself, and present yourself before your Lord in order to praise Him. The various positions you assume during prayer are the true example of the spirit of submission. The different things you recite remind you of the commitments you have to your creator. You seek

96

His guidance, ask Him again and again to help you avoid His wrath and to follow the Chosen Path. You recite from the book of the Lord and bear witness to the truth of the prophet. By your *salat,* you refresh your belief in the Day of Judgment and remember that you have to appear before your Master and give an account of your entire life. This is how your day starts. Then, after a few hours, you again submit before God and renew your commitment to Him. Here, you disassociate yourself from worldly engagements for a few moments and seek audience with your Maker. You actually communicate with the Lord of the Universe. This once again brings to the front of your mind the real role you have in life. Now, you go back to your occupations and after a few hours again present yourself before God. You cannot help but refocus your attention back on the demands made on you by your beliefs. When the sun sets and the darkness of the night begins to cover you, you again submit to the Almighty One so that you won't forget your duties in the midst of the approaching shadows of the night. After a few more hours, you again appear before your Lord, this being your last prayer of the day. Thus, before going to bed you renew your faith and prostrate before your true Master. It is in this manner that you complete your day. This is an intelligent and systematic way of approaching a form of worship.[1] The timing and frequency of the prayers never allows the real objective and mission of life to be lost sight of in the maze of worldly activities.

---

[1] Salat is a systematic way of worshipping God. The position of Islam is that God revealed a form of salat to each prophet. The form given to Muhammad by Him is precisely that practiced by the nearly one billion Muslims across the globe.

This systematic method of worship includes recitation of the Qur'an, repetition of selected words for praising Almighty God, standing, kneeling, sitting, prostrating, and other postures and movements. Basically, it is the Islamic way of communicating with God. Muslims believe that God, as the creator of the human body, knows best what is good for its spiritual as well as physical health, and salat is a systematic exercise program. It serves to mobilize body fluids, increases ranges of motion in joints, promotes the return of blood to the heart, and provides a minimal muscle tonus. By mobilizing body fluids through systematic contraction

(continued)

It is easy to understand how daily prayers strengthen the foundations of your faith. They prepare a person for living the life of goodness and obedience to God. This system of worship prepares pure hearts, advances the soul, and builds courage and determination within the individual.

Now let's see how this is achieved. You perform ablution[2] and do it in the way taught by the prophet. You also pray according to the instructions given by the prophet. Why do you do this? Simply because you believe that Muhammad is the prophet of God and regard it your absolute duty to follow him without question. Why don't you intentionally misrecite the Qur'an? Isn't it because you regard the book as the Word of God and deem it a sin to deviate from its script? In prayers, you recite many things silently. If you

---

(continued from previous page)

of muscles, salat serves to prevent stagnation of fluids within the tissues. A lack of static fluids helps prevent infections and actually cleanses the body down to the cellular level by increasing the excretion of harmful substances. Salat is an excellent way to increase ranges of motion in joints. The rhythmic flexion and extension of the body helps relax the ligaments and tendons attached to the joints, frees joint articulations (the place where two opposing bones of a joint meet) and increases the production of synovial fluid (the fluid which lubricates joint surfaces). These effects help prevent the joint from succumbing to degenerative disorders like arthritis, and make overall body mechanics more efficient. The various postures assumed in salat, as well as the rhythmic contraction of muscles, result in an increase in blood return to the heart. Some salat postures specifically allow a more physiologic and efficient drainage of blood from the brain, spinal cord, and legs to occur. The ultimate result of this is to increase both the removal of toxic wastes from and the delivery of nutrient material to all the organs and cells of the body.

Muscles and tendons are significantly affected by salat. By properly assuming its various postures, every major muscle of the body is affected. This effect is due to both muscular contraction and muscle stretch, the most optimal method for improving the tone and health of muscle tissue. It is interesting that only within the last decade have athletic authorities fully realized the importance of a program combining systematic, static stretch with eccentric and concentric muscle contraction. The salat instituted over 1400 years ago by Muhammad (peace be on him) provides precisely these effects. Some authorities even claim it to be a better exercise than jogging in some cases, and it has been described as the perfect sequence for providing the minimum daily requirement for exercise.

[2] This is the form of cleansing required before salat can be performed.

(continued)

do not recite, or if you make any deviation thereof, there is no one to check you. But you never do so intentionally. Why? Because you believe that God is ever watchful and He hears all that your recite. You believe He hears all things whether silent or spoken. What makes you perform prayer at places where there is no one to ask you if you offered them or even to see you offering them? Isn't it because of your belief that God is always looking at you? What makes you terminate your sweet sleep in the early hours of the morning to go to the mosque in the heat of the noon, or to leave your evening entertainments for the sake of prayers? What makes you leave important business and other occupational engagements in order to perform your prayers? Is it anything other than your sense of duty —your realization that you must fulfill your responsibility to the Lord, come what may? And why are you afraid of making a mistake in the postures of prayer? Because your heart is filled with the fear of God and you know you have to appear before Him on the Day of Judgment. You know that then you will have to give an account of your entire life. Now look! Can there be a better course of moral and spiritual training than prayers? It is this training which

---

(continued from previous page)
Ablution (*wudu* in Arabic) is the method used by a Muslim to prepare his body and soul before he presents himself to his Creator. It involves washing the hands, mouth, nose, face, ears, arms to the elbow and feet. Ablution cleanses those areas of the body most frequently exposed to the exterior environment. These areas tend to accumulate dirt and foreign particles, and it is these areas from which bacteria and other infectious organisms may be housed or transmitted.

The Western world has only recently discovered the benefits of proper hygiene. While for the West the attendance to bodily cleanliness has been in practice little more than 100 years, Muhammad (peace be on him) drilled home the importance of this to his followers over 1400 years ago. In 17th century England, bathing was regarded as an act of foolishness. People who bathed regularly were regarded as criminals by the state while the Church condemned them as sinners. In contrast, hundreds of years before this, Muhammad described physical cleanliness as a form of worshipping God, and was the first to establish basic scientific rules for improving the health and hygiene of the masses. Up until the late 1800's most surgeons regarded it as heresy to wash their hands prior to

(continued)

makes a man a perfect Muslim. It reminds him of his covenant with God, refreshes his faith in Him, and keeps the belief in the Day of Judgment ever present in his mind. It makes him follow the prophet and trains him to observe his duties. This is indeed a strict training for conforming one's practice to one's ideals. If a man's awareness of his duties to his Creator is so acute that he prizes them above everything else and keeps refreshing this awareness through *salat*, he would certainly stay clean in all his dealings. For, otherwise, he would be inviting the displeasure of God which he had all along set out to avoid. He will abide by the law of God in all affairs of life, just as he does

---

(continued from previous page)

performing an operation. The 1400 year old Islamic invention of washing the arms to the elbows and thoroughly cleansing the hands has only recently been made mandatory in hospitals, clinics, and nurseries in order to protect those susceptible to infectious diseases.

Since salat is performed several times a day, the hands, nose, and mouth must also be washed many times. These sites are notorious for both housing and spreading organisms responsible for infections. It is the mouth and nose especially wherein the greatest number of micro-organisms reside. In fact, modern medical institutions would greatly benefit by using the Islamic form of cleansing the nose which includes sniffing water into the nostrils, thus rinsing them out. The reason is that antibiotic-resistant organisms are frequently picked up from the air in hospitals and transmitted from the carrier's nasal passages to the susceptible individual. The result is often serious infection and even death in many cases. Also, sniffing water into the nostrils bathes the sinuses with water mist, literally acting to cleanse the sinal cavities. This serves two purposes. Water is nature's form of 'nasal decongestant', and such a procedure can be a therapy for the congested sinuses commonly associated with colds, hayfever, or the flu. It is well known that the primary mechanism leading to most upper respiratory infections is the accumulation of nasal and pharyngeal secretions. Due to this lack of fluid exchange and mobility, viral and bacterial organisms can multiply and cause a cold, flu, etc. Constant cleansing of the nose, throat, and mouth through ablution thus attacks the primary disease-initiating mechanism by promoting the flow and drainage of these secretions and by diluting the numbers of organisms found in these cavities.

The other benefits of this cleansing procedure are too numerous to properly address here. The major theme is this: God Almighty, the highest source of Purity, expects His creatures, His representatives, to be the best examples of purity and cleanliness in both body and soul. —
The Editors.

in his five daily prayers. This man can be relied upon in other fields of life as well, for if the shadows of sin or deceit approach him, he will try to avoid them. He will avoid them because the fear of His Lord is ever present in his heart. And if, even after such a vital training, a man misbehaves in other fields of life and disobeys the law of God, it can only be because of some intrinsic fault of his self.

When possible, prayers must be performed in congregation, especially the Friday prayer. This serves to bind the Muslims together on the basis of love and mutual understanding. It arouses a tremendous sense of unity within them, and builds them into a national fraternity. All Muslims pray in one congregation and this gives them a deep feeling of brotherhood. *Salat* is also a symbol of equality, for the poor and the rich, the low and the high, the rulers and the ruled, the educated and the uneducated, the black and the white, all stand in one row and prostrate before the same One God.

These are a few of the benefits we can derive from daily prayers. If we refuse to use them we, and only we, are the losers. Our avoiding prayers can only mean one of two things. Either we do not recognize *salat* as our duty or we recognize it as our duty and still avoid it. In the first case, our claim to Faith shall be a shameless lie, for if we refuse to take orders, we no longer acknowledge the Authority. In the second case, if we recognize the Authority and still flout His Commands, then we are the most unreliable of creatures that ever tread the earth. For if we can do this to the highest authority in the universe, what guarantee is there that we shall not do the same in our dealings with fellow human beings? And if double play overwhelms a society, what a hell of a discord it is bound to become!

FASTING

What prayer seeks to accomplish five times a day, fasting during the month of Ramadan (the ninth month of the lunar year) does once a year. During this period from dawn to dusk, we eat not a crumb of food nor drink a drop

101

of water, no matter how delicious the dish or how hungry or thirsty we feel. What is it that makes us voluntarily undergo such hardships? It is nothing but belief in God and the fear of Him and the day we will return to Him. Every moment during our fast we suppress our passions and desires and by so doing, proclaim the supremacy of the Law of God. This great test keeps us extremely conscious of our duties and so strengthens our faith. By denying ourselves of the most basic necessity of life, an unparalleled spirit of patience is built within us. Difficulty and discipline during this month bring us face to face with the realities of life and help us make our life during the rest of the year one of true subservience to God's Will.

Fasting also has an immense impact on society. All Muslims irrespective of status must fast during the same month. This brings into the open the true equality of men and thus goes a long way towards creating feelings of love and brotherhood among them. During Ramadhan, evil conceals itself, while good comes to the fore. The whole atmosphere is filled with cleanliness, righteousness, and purity.[3]

---

[3] The benefits of fasting are not limited to the spiritual sphere. It also has tremendous benefits for human health. Fasting in a well designed manner, that is abstaining from foodstuffs and drink for only a certain period during the day, can significantly affect health. Most diseases today are the result of excesses—therefore, the diseases of obesity, heart and arterial disease, and cancer are by far most common in the West. The health of Western societies is plainly plagued by its habit of overeating. Fasting interrupts this cycle. It serves to give the overburdened body, particularly the overworked digestive system, a rest. By resting the digestive tract, all body systems which depend on the activities of the food digestive process, whether circulatory, kidney, muscular, or skeletal, are relieved from the constant burden (at least as seen in Western society) of breaking down and utilizing excessive foodstuffs. Thus, body energies are diverted from the highly energy-requiring breakdown and assimilation of nutrients to the often neglected processes of synthesis and cleansing. By cleansing is meant the active process of removing waste products and substances which are detrimental to health. These are substances which the body cannot fully cope with when most of its energy is channelled into dealing with digestion. This includes the substances

(continued)

ZAKAT

The third obligation is *zakat*. Every Muslim whose financial conditions are above a specified minimum must pay annually 2½% of his cash balance and any other liquid assets such as gold, silver, bonds, etc. The collected wealth is used for such causes as supporting the improverished and unemployed. Or it may be used to help a needy individual—a poor man, a traveler, a new convert to Islam, a needy student. It can also be used for supporting the Islamic State. Its goal is to provide a more balanced distribution of wealth, theoretically eliminating the extremes in wealth and poverty that plague today's world. This 2½% is the minimum. The more you pay, the greater the reward that the All-Merciful God shall bestow on you.

The money paid as *zakat* is not something God needs or receives. He is above any want or desire. He, in His immeasurable Mercy, promises us tremendous rewards if we help our brethren. But there is one basic condition for being so rewarded. It is that when we pay in the name of God, we shall not expect nor demand any worldly gains

(continued from previous page)

which collect on arterial walls, commonly known as "hardening of the arteries". In truth, this is usually not an actual hardening but is an accumulation of fatty substances on the inside of the artery. By not eating or drinking for several hours each day over a month-long period, the body is able to mobilize much of this 'greasing' off the arterial walls, thereby promoting a decrease in blood pressure and pulse, and an increase in the overall health and efficiency of the heart.

In a similar way, fasting helps the body remove various toxic substances. Many of these substances can potentially cause cancer. Fasting accomplishes this by increasing the energies channeled to the two primary excretory organs, the liver and kidney, which eliminate these wastes in the urine and feces. It may also prevent cancer by decreasing the constant stress placed on the digestive organs, resting these organs, and thereby directly reducing their tendency toward cancerous degeneration. Here it must be noted that the epithelial cells of the digestive tract are the most rapidly growing cells in the body, and have the fastest rate of being destroyed and renewed. Cancer is a disease of uncontrolled growth of cells. The more 'rest' this digestive machinery is given, the less likely it is to become cancerous. - The Editors.

from the persons receiving our gifts nor aim at making our names as philanthropists.

Zakat is as basic to Islam as other forms of worship like prayer and fasting. Its main importance lies in the fact that it fosters in us the qualities of sacrifice and rids us of selfishness and greed. Islam wants only those people who are ready to give in God's way from their hard-earned wealth willingly and without expecting any temporal or personal gain. It has nothing to do with misers. A true Muslim shall, when the call comes, sacrifice all his belongings in the way of God, for *zakat* has already trained him for such sacrifice.

The Muslim society has a tremendous amount to gain from the institution of *zakat*. It is the duty of every well-to-do Muslim to help his less fortunate, impoverished brothers. His wealth is not to be spent solely for his comfort and luxury—there are rightful claimants on his wealth. They are the society's widows and orphans, the poor and invalid, and those who have the ability but lack the means by which to get employment. They are those who have talents and intelligence but not the money by which to use these abilities. He who does not recognize the right such members of his community have on his wealth is indeed cruel. For there could be no greater cruelty than to fill one's own coffers while thousands die of hunger or suffer the agonies of unemployment. Islam is a sworn enemy of such selfishness and greed. Disbelievers, devoid of feelings of universal love, know only to preserve wealth and to add to it by lending it out on interest. Islam's teachings are the exact opposite of this attitude. It tells a person to share his wealth with others and help them stand on their own two feet so they can become productive members of society.

PILGRIMAGE (HAJJ)

Pilgrimage to Mecca is the fourth basic form of worship. It is obligatory only for those who can afford it and that too only once in a lifetime. Mecca today stands at the site of a small house which prophet Abraham built for the worship of God. God Almighty rewarded him by calling it His House and by making it the center towards which all must face when performing *salat*.

Our visit to this place is not supposed to be a courtesy call. Even this pilgrimage has its practices and its conditions to be fulfilled. It also seeks to build purity and goodness in us. When we undertake the pilgrimage, we must suppress our passions, refrain from bloodshed, and be pure in our words and deeds. God promises rewards for our sincerity and submissiveness.

The pilgrimage is, in a way, the biggest form of worship. For unless a man really loves God, he would never undertake such a long journey leaving all his near and dear ones behind. Then, this pilgrimage is unlike any other journey. Here his thoughts are concentrated on God, his inner core vibrates with the spirit of intense devotion. When he reaches the holy place, he finds the atmosphere laden with purity and godliness; he is visiting the places which bear witness to the glory of Islam. All this leaves a deep impression on his mind, which he carries to his last breath.

There are many benefits which Muslims can gain from this pilgrimage. Mecca is the center towards which the Muslims must converge each year. They meet and discuss topics of common interest, and create and refresh within the concept that all Muslims are equal. They regenerate their fundamental belief that each Muslim deserves the love and sympathy of all his brothers regardless of where they came from or to what race they belong. Thus, pilgrimage unites the Muslims of the world into one international brotherhood.

DEFENSE OF ISLAM

The defense of Islam is not a fundamental belief but its importance has been repeatedly emphasized in the Qur'an and Sunnah. It is essentially a test of our sincerity as believers in Islam. If we do not defend a friend of ours against plots or assaults from his enemies, nor care for his needs, we are indeed false pretenders of friendship. In the same way, if we profess belief in Islam, we must jealously guard and uphold the prestige of Islam. Our sole guide for our conduct must be the interests of Muslims at large and the service of Islam in the face of which all our personal considerations must sink low.

JIHAD

Jihad is a part of this overall defense of Islam. Jihad means to struggle to the utmost of one's capacity. A man who exerts himself physically or mentally or spends his wealth in the cause of God is indeed engaged in *jihad.* But in the language of the Divine Law, this word is used specifically for the war that is waged solely in the name of God against those who perpetrate oppression as enemies of Islam. This supreme sacrifice is the responsibility of all Muslims. If, however, a section of the Muslims offer themselves for participating in *jihad,* the whole community is absolved of its responsibility. But if none comes forward, everyone is held guilty. This concession vanishes for the citizens of an Islamic State when it is attacked by a non-Muslim power. In this case, everybody must come forward for *jihad.* If the country attacked doesn't have enough strength to fight back, then it is the duty of the neighboring Muslim countries to help her. If even they fail, then the Muslims of the whole world must fight the common enemy. In all these cases, *jihad* is as much a primary duty as are daily prayers or fasting. One who avoids it is a sinner. His very claim to being a Muslim is doubtful. He is plainly a hypocrite who fails in the test of sincerity and all his acts of worship are a sham, a worthless, hollow show of devotion.

CHAPTER SIX

FAITH AND DIVINE LAW

Until now, the concept of faith has been discussed. We now come to a discussion of Divine Law. But let us first be sure we know the difference between Faith and Divine Law.

DISTINCTION BETWEEN FAITH AND DIVINE LAW

In the earlier chapters we said that all the prophets propagated Islam. This is a very basic fact. These men propagated a system of life requiring faith in God with all His attributes. They told people to believe in the Day of Judgment, and in the numerous prophets and books sent by God. In other words, they asked the people to live a life of obedience to their Lord. They asked them to live that life which would make them at peace with their Creator. This is what makes up Faith, the common teaching of all prophets.

Besides faith, there is Divine Law or the detailed code of conduct covering all aspects of life. The Divine Law is made of rules for the methods of worship, standards of morality and of life, laws that permit and prohibit, and rules that judge between right and wrong. This law has been undergoing amendments throughout time. Though each prophet had the same Faith, he brought with him a different Divine Law that suited the conditions of his specific people and time. This served the purpose of training different people over the ages. It helped each society build a better civilization by equipping them with higher morals. But the process ended with the advent of Muhammad (peace be on him). It was this man who brought with him the final system which applies to all mankind for all times to come. Faith and belief have undergone no change. However, all previous Divine Laws stand abrogated in view of the comprehensive Divine Law which Muhammad (peace be on him) brought with him. This is the climax of the great process of training that was started from the beginning of man's existence.

We draw upon two major sources in order to acquaint ourselves with the Divine Law. They are the Qur'an and Hadith. The Qur'an is the Divine revelation—each and every word of it is from God. The Hadith is a collection of the instructions issued by the last prophet. It describes his conduct and behavior. This was preserved by the people who lived around him, who were in constant touch with him, or by those who were given this information by eyewitnesses. These traditions were later collected and preserved by scholars and compiled in book form. Of these, the collections made by Malik, Bukhari, Muslim, Tirmizi, Abu Dawud, Nasa'i, and Ibn Majah are the most authentic.

JURISPRUDENCE (FIQH)

The leading legists of the past compiled a detailed law derived from the Qur'an and Hadith. This law is known as jurisprudence. It cares for the many problems that arise in daily life. Thus, the Muslims are forever indebted to those men of learning who devoted their lives to gaining a mastery of the Qur'an and Hadith and thereby made it easy for every Muslim to fashion his life according to the requirements of the Divine Law. They alone made it possible for Muslims all over the world to easily be able to follow the system of God, even though their achievements in religion are such that they themselves could never give a correct, authentic interpretation of the Qur'an or Hadith.

Though originally, a large number of religious leaders devoted themselves to the task, now only four major schools of thought remain. They are:

1. School of Hanifi: This is the jurisprudence compiled by Abu Hanifa with the assistance of other scholars.

2. School of Maliki: This jurisprudence was established by Malik Ashabi.

3. School of Shafi'i: Founded by Muhammad Shafi'i.

4. School of Hanbali: Founded by Ahmad Hanbal.

All these were given their final form within 200 years of the time of Muhammad. The differences that appear in the four schools are but the natural outcome of the fact that truth is many-sided. When different persons interpret a given event, they come out with explanations according to their varying abilities and levels of understanding. What gives these various schools of thought the authenticity that is associated with them is the unquestionable integrity of their respective founders and the authenticity of the method of collection and preservation they used. That is why all Muslims, whatever school they belong to, regard all four schools as correct and true. Though the authenticity of all of them goes unchallenged, one can follow only one of them in one's life. Even so, there is also a group of people of the Hadith who believe that those who have the required knowledge should directly approach the Qur'an and Hadith for guidance, and those who don't have such knowledge should follow whoever they choose in regard to a particular issue.

MYSTICISM (TASAWWUF)

Jurisprudence deals with the apparent and observable conduct, the fulfilling of a duty in practice. The field concerning itself with the spirit of conduct is know as *tasawwuf* (mysticism). For example, when we perform *salat,* jurisprudence judges us only by the fulfillment of physical requirements, such as cleansing, facing towards the *Kaaba,* and the timing and number of units. Mysticism, on the other hand, judges our salat by our concentration, devotion, and purification of our souls. It judges the effect *salat* has on our morals and manners. Thus, true Islamic mysticism is the measure of our spirit of obedience and sincerity, while jurisprudence governs our carrying out of commands to the last detail. An act of worship devoid of spirit, though correct in procedure, is like a man handsome in appearance but defective in character. An act of worship full of spirit, but defective in execution is like a man noble in character but deformed in appearance.

This clarifies the relation between jurisprudence and mysticism. It is the misfortune of the Muslims that as they sank in knowledge with the passage of time, as they became poor examples of what their religion taught them, they succumbed to the misguided philosophies of nations which were then dominant. They partook of these philosophies and patched Islam with their perverted ideas. They mixed the pure religion of God with falsehoods created by man.

They polluted the pure spring of Islamic mysticism with absurdities that could in no way be justified by any stretch of the imagination. Nothing in the Qur'an or Sunnah could be found to justify them. With time, a group of Muslims appeared who proclaimed themselves immune to and above the requirements of Divine Law. These people are totally ignorant of Islam, for Islam cannot stand for any mysticism which loosens itself from salat, fasting, zakat, and hajj. Mysticism, in the true sense, is but an intense love of God Almighty and of Muhammad (peace be on him). Such love requires strict obedience to their commands. Any who deviates from the Divine commands makes a false claim of his love for God and His messenger.

110

CHAPTER SEVEN

THE PRINCIPLES OF DIVINE LAW

Our discussion of the fundamentals of Islam will remain incomplete if we do not review the law of Islam. We must study its basic principles. We must try to visualize the type of man and society which Islam wants to produce. In this chapter we propose to study the principles of Divine Law so our picture of Islam can become complete and so we can appreciate the superiority of the Islamic way of life. The Divine Law: ITS MEANING AND SIGNIFICANCE

Man has been endowed with countless powers and skills and Providence has been very bountiful to him in this respect. He has intelligence and wisdom, will and free choice, the ability to see, speak, taste, touch, and hear. He has powers of strength, quickness, and agility, passions of love, fear, and anger. All these are of the utmost use to him and none of them is unnecessary or in excess. These faculties have been given to man because he needs them desperately. They are indispensible to him. His life and success depend upon the proper use of these powers. They are given to him by God and are meant for his service and unless they are used in full measure, life cannot become worth living.

God also provided man with all those means and resources which were needed to put his natural abilities to function and to achieve the fulfillment of his needs. The human body has been so constructed that it is man's greatest tool in his struggle for the fulfillment of the goals of life. Then there is the world in which man lives. His environment and surroundings contain resources of every description, resources which he uses for the achievement of his objectives. Nature and all that is within her have been harnessed for him and he can make every conceivable use of them. There are also other men of his kind so that they may cooperate with each other in the reconstruction of a better and more prosperous world. Now reflect deeply over this phenomenon. These powers and resources have been given to you so they may be used for the good of others. They have been created for your good and are not meant to harm or destroy you. Their function is to enrich life with the good and pure and not to throw it into jeopardy. Thus, the proper use of these powers is that which makes them beneficial to you. Even if there be some harm, it must not exceed the unavoidable minimum. This alone would amount to the proper use of these resources. Any use which results in waste or destruction would be wrong, unreasonable, and uncalled for. If you do something that causes destruction or injury, that would be a mistake pure and simple. Or if your actions hurt others and make you a nuisance to them, that would clearly be foolishness. It would be a total misuse of God-given powers. Such actions are flagrantly unreasonable, for it is human reason itself which demands that destruction and injury must be avoided and the path of gain and profit be pursued. Any deviation from this would obviously be a wrong course.

Keeping this in mind, when we look at human beings, we find there are two kinds of people. First, there are those who knowingly misuse the skill God gave them and through this misuse, waste the resources, injure their own vital interests, and hurt other people. Second are those who are sincere and earnest but make mistakes because of ignorance. Those who intentionally misuse their powers are wicked and generate evil and deserve the powerful club of law for their control and reform. Those who err because of ignorance need knowledge and guidance, so they can see the Right Path and make the best use of their abilities. It is this system of behavior—the Divine Law—which God revealed to mankind that fulfills this very need.

The Divine Law makes God's regulations very clear and specific and thus provides guidance for the regulation of

112

how man should live. Its objective is to show man the *best way* and provide him with the method to fulfill his needs in the most successful and beneficial way. The Law of God is out and out for your benefit. Nothing in it tends to waste your talents or suppress your passions and desires. Nothing in it seeks to kill your normal urges and emotions. It does not plead for asceticism. It does not say: Abandon the world, give up all ease and comfort, leave your homes and wander about in plains and mountains and jungles without bread or cloth, putting yourself to inconveniences and self-annihilation. No, certainly not. This viewpoint has no relevance to Islam, for Islam is that system created by the All-Knowing God for the benefit of mankind. Its laws are created by that very being Who harnessed everything for man's use. He would not like to ruin His creation. He has not given man any power that is useless, nor has He created anything in the entire universe which is not of service to man. Rather, it is His explicit will that the universe—this grand workshop with its diversified activities —should go on functioning smoothly so that man—the prize of creation—can make the most productive use of his potentials. It is His will that man should use everything provided for him in the earth and high heavens. He should use them in a way that he and his fellow human beings can reap handsome prizes from them. Never should they intentionally or unintentionally harm any of God's creation. The Divine Law is made to guide man's direction in this respect. It forbids all that is harmful to man and allows all that is useful and beneficial to him.

What this Law basically says is that man has the right, and in some cases it is his absolute duty, to fulfill all his genuine needs and desires. He should make every conceivable effort to promote his interests and achieve success and happiness. But, and it is an important but, he should do all this in a way that the interests of others are not jeopardized. No harm should befall others as they work towards their objectives. All possible social cohesion, assistance, and cooperation should be accomplished in the achievement of their objectives. Sometimes there are things in which good and evil or gain and loss are irreversibly bound together. The attitude of the Divine Law in relation to the above is to accept a little harm for the sake of gaining greater benefits. It also allows for sacrificing some benefit to avoid greater harm. This is the basic approach of the Divine Law in all fields of life.

Now we know that man's knowledge is limited. Every man in every age does not by himself know what is good and what is evil, what is helpful and what is harmful to him. The sources of human knowledge are too limited to provide him with the clear truth. This is why God has spared man of the risks of trial and error. This is why He revealed the law which is the correct and complete system of life for the entire human race. The merits and truths of this system are becoming more apparent with the passage of time. A few centuries ago, many of its advantages were hidden to the eye. They have now become clear with the increase in knowledge. Even today, many do not appreciate all the merits of this system. But as knowledge progresses, new light is thrown on them and brings their superiority into clear perspective. The world has no choice but to drift towards the Divine System—many of those who refused to accept it now, after centuries of gropings and trials, being obliged to adopt some of its provisions. Those who denied the truth of the revelation and pinned all hope on unguided reason, after committing blunders and courting bitter experience, are adopting in one way or the other the rules of Divine Law. But after what a loss!—and even then they are not using it in its entirety. In contrast, there are people who put their trust in God's prophets, accept what they say, and adopt the Divine Law they taught. They may not be aware of all the merits of a certain instruction, but on the whole, they accept a code which is the outcome of true knowledge. They accept a system of laws which saves them from the evils and blunders of ignorance. They put their trust in a system of truth rather than placing their hopes on trial and error. Such are the people who are on the right track and are bound to succeed.

DIVINE LAW: RIGHTS AND OBLIGATIONS

The scheme of life which Islam envisages consists of a set of rights and obligations. Broadly speaking, the law of Islam imposes four kinds of rights and obligations on every man. They are: 1) the rights of God upon man, 2) man's rights upon himself, 3) the rights of other people over him, and 4) the rights of those powers and resources which God has put at man's service. These rights and obligations form a very important part of Islam. It is the duty of every true Muslim to understand their significance and put them into practice earnestly. All of them have been discussed clearly and in detail by the Divine Law. The method by which these obligations can be performed is also provided. This is so that all of them can be put into practice at the same time and none of them gets violated or trampled under foot. Now we shall briefly discuss these rights and obligations so an idea of the Islamic system of life can be formed.

1. THE RIGHTS OF GOD

First we must study the grounds on which Islam bases the relationship of man to his Creator. The most important right God has on us is that man should have faith in Him Alone. He should acknowledge His authority and associate none with Him. This is epitomized in the statement: *la ilaha illallah* (there is no other God but God).

The second right God has on us is that we accept without question and follow His guidance—the system He revealed to man—and seek His pleasure with all the energy we have. We fulfill this right by believing in His prophet and by accepting his guidance and teachings.

The third right He has on us is that we obey Him with complete honesty, and without reservation. We fulfill the needs of this by following God's law as contained in the Qur'an and Sunnah.

The fourth right He has is that we worship Him. This is done through the acts of worship discussed earlier.

These important duties precede all other rights and as

such they are performed even at the cost of some sacrifice to other rights and duties. For example, in performing *salat* or in fasting, you must sacrifice many personal rights. A man has to undergo hardships and sacrifices when correctly performing his duties to his Creator. He has to get up early in the morning for prayer, and so must sacrifice his sleep and rest. During the day, he often puts off many important works and gives some of his time just to worship his Maker. In the month of fasting, he braces hunger and puts up with many inconveniences just to please his Lord. By paying *zakat,* he loses some of his wealth and demonstrates that the love of God is over and above everything else, and that the love of wealth cannot come in its way. In pilgrimage, he undergoes sacrifices of wealth and bears the troubles of travel. And in *jihad,* he sacrifices money, material, and all that he has—even his own life.

When it comes to the rights of God, fulfilling your duty may mean that others lose some of their rights. You too may have some of your interests hurt. A laborer has to leave his work when the time of *salat* arrives and attend to the worship of his Lord. A businessman must stop his business long enough to undertake the pilgrimage to Mecca.

In *jihad,* man takes away life and gives it solely in the cause of God. The right God has on us makes us sacrifice many things which we have in our control like wealth, time, and resource. But the way the infinitely wise God has constructed the Divine Law, sacrifice of the rights of others has been reduced to the barest minimum. God has thus granted us a great deal of leeway so we can easily fulfill the rights He has upon us. Look at the flexibility He has given us so we can fulfill the obligation of *salat.* If no water is available for ablution, you can perform *tayammum* (dry ablution). If you are traveling, you can shorten the *salat.* If you are ill and cannot stand in prayer, you can perform it while sitting, and if you are too sick to sit, you can do it lying down.

Fasting follows the same rule. If you are traveling or are sick, you don't have to fast and can make up any missed days at a more convenient time. Women are exempted from fasting when they are pregnant, during their menstrual period, or during lactation. The fast must be broken at the appointed time, and without any delay. Any delay in it is disapproved. There is permission to eat and drink from sunset up to the break of dawn. Optional fasts are highly valued by God and He is pleased with them. But He doesn't want you to fast continuously and make yourself too weak to adequately perform your ordinary occupation.

Now look at the case of *zakat;* only the minimum rate has been fixed by God and man is left free to spend as much more as he likes in the cause of God. If the minimum amount is given, the basic duty is fulfilled. But if more is spent in charity, one seeks even more of God's pleasure. But here again He does not like us to sacrifice all that we own in charity. Nor are we to deny ourselves or our relatives the rightful pleasures and comforts of life. He does not want us to impoverish ourselves. We are commanded to be moderate in charity.

Then look at pilgrimage. Only those who are physically or financially able are required to perform it. The poor health of some and the impoverished conditions of others doesn't allow them to perform it. God understands these problems and in His mercy makes an exception for such people. For those capable of it, it is only required once in a lifetime, and this in any year that is convenient. If there is a war or any other situation which poses a risk of life, it can be postponed. Moreover, the parent's permission has been made an essential condition so that in their later years they won't suffer any discomfort in your absence. All these things clearly show the importance God Almighty has given to the rights of others as contrasted to His own rights.

The greatest sacrifice made in the way of God is *jihad.* In it man sacrifices not only his own life and belongings, but destroys those of others as well. But the Islamic principle is that we should suffer a lesser loss in order to save ourselves from a greater one. What comparison would the loss of some lives—even if it were some thousands or

117

more—be to the calamity that would befall mankind as the result of the victory of evil over good. What comparison would it be to the tremendous anguish mankind would suffer if falsehood overtook truth, and if aggressive atheism won over the religion of God. Not only would the religion of God be eliminated, but the world would become the abode of evil, corruption, and perversion. Life would be disrupted from within and without. In order to prevent this greater evil, God has commanded us to sacrifice our lives and property for His pleasure. Yet He has forbidden unnecessary bloodshed. Women, children, the crippled, the old, and the sick and wounded should under no circumstances be harmed. We would be guilty of a tremendous sin if we injure them. His order is to fight only those who rise to fight. God tells us not to cause unnecessary destruction of even the enemies' lands. Trees are not to be cut down, crops are not to be burned, and homes are not to be looted and destroyed. The defeated must be dealt with fairly and honorably. We are instructed to observe any treaties made with the enemy and must stop fighting when they do. We must not fight them any longer once they stop their aggressive anti-Islamic activities. Thus Islam allows for only the minimum sacrifice of life, property, and the rights of others during the performance of the rights of God.

II. THE RIGHTS OF THE SELF

Next come man's personal rights, i.e. the rights each individual has on himself.

The fact is man is more cruel and unjust to himself than to any other creature. On the surface it seems astonishing. How can man be unjust to himself particularly when he finds that he loves himself the most? How can he be his own enemy? It doesn't seem to make sense. But deeper reflection shows that it contains a large element of truth.

The greatest weakness man has is that when he is confronted by an overpowering desire, instead of resisting it, he succumbs to it. Then, in its gratification, he knowingly brings great harm to himself. There is the man who takes to drinking. He becomes mad after it and continues indulging in it at cost of money, health, reputation, and everything else he has. Another is so fond of eating, that he overeats to the point of spoiling his health and endangering his life. Yet another becomes a slave of his sexual appetites and ruins himself in over-indulgence. Still another seeks spiritual elevations. He suppresses his genuine desires and refuses to fulfil his natural physical requirements. Doing away with food, clothing, and shelter, he leaves his home and retires into the mountains and jungles. He believes the world is not meant for him and he hates everything in it. These are just a few examples of man's tendency to go to extremes and get lost in any given field. There are many other instances where people adjust poorly to everyday life and there is no need to expound on them here.

Islam stands for the welfare of man and its avowed objective is to establish a balanced life, a life which follows a middle road. Islam wants to avoid a life which follows the extremes at either end. This is why the Divine Law clearly declares that your own self has certain rights upon you.

This Law forbids the use of all things which injure man's physical, mental, or moral existence. It forbids drinking blood or intoxicating drinks. We are told not to eat unclean animals. Pork, beasts of prey, poisonous animals, and the carcass are banned. The main reason is that all these have harmful effects upon the physical, moral, and intellectual life of man. While forbidding these things, Islam makes legal for man the use of all clean, healthy and useful things. Islam tells him not to deprive his body of clean food, for man's body has a right upon him. Islam forbids nudity and orders man to use decent and dignified dress. It demands that he work for a living. It disapproves of laziness and makes it clear that the Muslim who works hard to earn his living is better than one who does little and earns nothing. The true message of the Divine Law is that man should use both the powers God has given him and the resources He has spread in the world for his comfort and welfare.

Islam does not believe in the suppression of even sexual desires. It tells man to regulate these desires by seeking their fulfillment in marriage. It forbids him from persecuting himself, from denying himself the rightful comforts and pleasures of life.

To become elevated spiritually, or to seek nearness to God, it is not necessary to abandon this world. To become saved in the life to come, there is no need to negate the life of this world. Instead, the true trial of life lies within this world and should remain in its midst and follow the divine system here in it. The road to success lies only in adhering to the Divine Law in the midst of life's complexities and not outside it.

Islam totally forbids suicide and impresses upon man that life belongs to God. It is like a trust which God has bestowed upon man for a certain period of time. He gave life to each individual so he could make the best use of it —it is not meant to be spoiled and destroyed in a foolish manner. Suicide is the most outrageous and ridiculous manifestation of man neglecting the rights of his self.

III. THE RIGHTS OF OTHER MEN

Even though the Divine Law has told man to fulfil his personal needs, he must not seek their fulfillment in such a way that the rights of other people are violated. The Divine Law seeks to strike a balance between the rights of individuals and the rights of the society. This is so that no conflict will arise between the two and so all will cooperate in establishing the law of God.

Islam strongly forbids the telling of a lie for it defiles the liar, harms other people, and is a source of menace to society. It has totally forbidden theft, bribery, forgery, cheating, interest, and usury. The reason for this is whatever man gains by this means is really obtained by causing loss and injury to others. Backbiting, tale-telling, slandering, malignment, gambling, lottery, speculation and all games of chance have been prohibited for in all of them one gains at the cost of thousands of others losing. All forms of exploitive commerce in which one party alone is the winner have been prohibited. Monopoly hoarding, blackmarketing, holding of land from cultivation and all other forms of individual and social aggrandizement have been outlawed. Murder, debauchery, the spreading of mischief and disorder, and destruction have been made crimes. They are made crimes because no one has the right to take away the life and property of another just so he can gain some personal gratification. Adultery, fornication and unnatural sexual indulgence have been strictly prohibited. It is common knowledge that these practices not only violate morality and impair the health of their perpetrator, but also spread corruption and immorality in society. They cause venereal diseases and ruin public health. This leads to the degeneration of the health and morals of the future generations. Human relationships are upset, and the very fabric of the cultural and social structure of the community are destroyed. Islam wants to eliminate, root and branch, such abominable crimes.

Each of these limits have been imposed upon man by Islam to prevent him from encroaching upon the rights of others. Islam doesn't want man to become so selfish and egotistical that he unashamedly assails the rights of others and violates all standards of decency just for the attainment of a few mental or physical pleasures. Nor does it allow him to crucify the interests of others in order to gain personal rights. The Islamic law so regulates life that the welfare of every person can be achieved. But for the sake of the welfare and cultural advancement of man, some negative restrictions are not by themselves sufficient. In a truly peaceful and prosperous society, it is not enough that there be regulations to stop people from violating others' rights. It is also necessary that people work together on a common format. They should establish relationships and social institutions which contribute towards the welfare of all. By this they can establish an ideal society. The Divine Law guides us in respect to this as well. Here is a brief summary of those rules of Islamic Law which throw light on this aspect of life.

The family is the cradle of man. Herein is where man's most important characteristics are built. For this reason, it is not only the cradle of man but is the cradle of civilization as well. The Divine Law contains specific rules concerning the family. A family consists of the husband, wife, and their children. The rules concerning the family are very explicit. Man is assigned the responsibility of earning and providing the necessities of life for his wife and children. He must protect them from all the difficulties and problems of life. The wife is assigned the duty of managing the household. Here she must train and bring up the children in the best possible manner. She must provide her husband and children with the greatest possible love and comfort. As for the children, it is their duty to respect and obey their parents and when they grow up, to serve them and provide for their needs. In order to make the household a well managed and disciplined institution, Islam has adopted the following measures:

(a) The husband has been made the head of the family. No institution can work smoothly unless there is a chief administrator in it. To have a school without a principle or a city without a mayor is unthinkable. If there is no one in control of an institution, nothing but chaos would result. If every person in a family went his own way, nothing but confusion would prevail. If the husband goes in one direction and the wife in another, the future of the children would be ruined. There must be someone serving as the head of the family so that discipline is maintained. In this way, the family becomes an ideal institution of society. By giving this position to the husband, Islam makes the family a disciplined primary unit of civilization, a model for society as a whole.

(b) This head of the family has further been burdened with other responsibilities. It is his duty to earn the living, and carry out those tasks which are performed outside the household. It has freed woman from extra household duties and assigned them all on the shoulders of the husband. She has been relieved from having to perform tasks outside the house so she can devote herself to indoor duties.

The reason is that now she can put all her energies into the maintenance of the household and in the rearing of children —the future guardians of the nation. Islam does not want to tax them doubly: to rear children, maintain the household, earn a living, and do outside jobs as well is asking too much of her. That obviously would be an injustice. Islam, therefore, produces a functional distribution between the sexes.

But this does not mean that women are not allowed to go out of the house. This is not the case. Women are allowed to go out when necessary. The law has specified the home as her *special* field of work and has stressed the great value attained if women attend to the improvement of home life. Whenever they have to go out, they can do so after observing certain formalities.

The general rule is that the sphere of the family widens through blood-relations and marriage connections. To bind together the members of the family into one unit, to keep their relations close and healthy, and to make each of them a source of support, strength and contentment to the other, Islam has provided certain basic rules. These rules may be summed up as follows:

1. Marriage between persons who have the closest association with each other has been prohibited. Relations between whom marriage is forbidden are: mother and son, father and daughter, step-father and step-daughter, step-mother and step-son, brother and sister, foster brother and foster sister, paternal uncle and his niece, aunt (father's or mother's sister) and her nephew, maternal uncle and his niece, mother-in-law and her son-in-law, and father-in-law and his daughter-in-law. This prohibition strengthens the bonds of the family and makes relations between these relatives absolutely pure. They can mix with each other without restraint and with sincere affection.

2. Beyond the limits of the forbidden marriages, matrimonial relations can occur between members of related families so to bind them still closer. Marriage connections between families which are freely associated with each

other, and which therefore know each other's habits, customs, and traditions, are generally successful. Therefore, the Divine Law not only permits them, but also encourages and prefers marriage between related families to those of entirely strange families (though this is not forbidden).

3. In a group of related families, there usually coexist the rich and the poor, the prosperous and the destitute. The Islamic principle is that a man's relatives have the greatest right on him. There is great respect for the tie between relatives. Muslims must respect this bond in every possible way. To be disloyal to one's relatives and to be negligent of their rights is a great sin and God has disapproved of it. If a relative becomes poor, or is beset with some trouble, it is the duty of his rich and prosperous relatives to help him. In *zakat* and other charities, special regard for the rights of relatives has been enjoined.

4. The law of inheritance is so constructed in Islam that the property left by the deceased cannot become concentrated at any one place. It is distributed in a way that all near relatives get their shares. Son, daughter, wife, husband, father, mother, brother, and sister are the nearest and their share in inheritance comes first. If these relatives are absent, shares are given to the next nearest relatives. Therefore, after a man dies, his wealth is distributed among his relatives and a fatal blow is struck at the capitalistic concentration of wealth. The law of Islam is of unique excellence, and other nations are now taking leaves out of it. But the sad irony is that the Muslims themselves are not fully aware of its revolutionary potential and, in ignorance, many of them are not putting it into practice. In several parts of the Muslim world, daughters are being deprived of their share in inheritance. This is a palpable injustice and a flagrant violation of the Qur'an's clear guidelines on this matter.

After the family comes man's relations with his friends, neighbors, fellow citizens, and persons with whom he comes into constant contact. Islam recognizes these relationships and tells a Muslim to treat them all honestly, equitably, and courteously. It tells the believers to be careful not to hurt others' feelings, to avoid indecent and abusive language, and to help each other. They are to take care of the sick, support the destitute, and assist the needy and crippled. They must sympathize with the people stricken by trouble or disaster. They must look after the orphans and widows, feed the hungry, clothe the under-clad, and help the unemployed in seeking employment. Islam says that if God has given you wealth and riches, don't squander it on luxurious frivolities. It has prohibited the use of gold and silver vessels, to wear costly silken dresses, and to waste money on useless ventures and extravagant luxuries. This injunction of the Divine Law is based on the principle that no man should be allowed to squander upon himself wealth that can maintain thousands of human beings. It is cruel and unjust that money which can be used to feed the starving humanity be tossed away in useless or extravagant decorations, exhibitions, and fireworks. Islam does not want to deprive a man of his wealth and belongings. What one has earned or inherited is beyond doubt his own property. Islam recognizes his right and allows him to enjoy it and make the best use of it. It also suggests that if you are wealthy, you should have better dress, better housing, and a decent living. But Islam wants to make sure that in all of man's activities, the human element is not lost sight of. What Islam totally disapproves of is conceited self-centeredness. It disapproves of egotistical thinking which leads to neglecting the welfare of others and gives birth to exaggerated individualism. It wants the entire society to prosper, not merely a few stray individuals. It instills in the minds of its followers social consciousness and suggests them to live a simple, sparing life. They should avoid excess in every aspect of life and strive to follow a middle road. But they are to fulfill their needs, while keeping in mind the needs of others. They should not even neglect the needs of their fellow citizens and should treat them as if they were blood brothers. This is what Islam wants to achieve.

Thus far, we have discussed the nature of man's relationship with his closer circles. Now look at the wider perspective and see what kind of community Islam wants to establish. Everyone who embraces Islam not only enters the fold of the religion, but also becomes a member of the Islamic community. The Divine Law contains certain rules of behavior for relationships on a wider basis as well. These rules assure that the Muslims work together and help each other to perform what is good and forbids what is harmful and evil. Rules are set up to make sure that no wrong creeps into their society. Some of these rules are as follows:

1. To preserve the moral life of the nation and to ensure that the society evolves on healthy lines, free mingling of the sexes has been prohibited. Islam wants there to be a functional division between the sexes. It provides different spheres of activity for both of them. Outside the limits of the nearest relatives between whom marriage is forbidden, men and women have been asked not to mix freely with each other and when they come into contact they should do so with proper dress. When women leave their homes, they should use simple dress and go out properly covered. Only in genuine necessity can they uncover, and there too they must re-cover when that necessity expires. Along with this, men have been asked not to look upon women by keeping a low gaze and avoiding staring at them. If someone accidentally happens to look at them, he should turn away the eye. To stare at them is wrong and to seek their acquaintance is worse. It is the duty of both men and women to look after their personal morality and purge their soul of all impurities. Marriage is the proper form of sexual relationship and no one should attempt to overstep this limit or even think of any sexual freedom. Man's mind should be completely cleansed from such perverse ideas.

2. People are encouraged to wear decent and respectable dress. No man should expose his body from the knees to the navel. Nor should a woman expose any part of her body except her face and hands to anyone other than her husband. To keep these parts covered is the religious duty of every man and woman. Through this directive, Islam wants to cultivate in its followers a deep sense of modesty and purity. It wants to suppress all forms of immodesty, lewdness, and moral deviation.

3. Islam does not approve of pastimes, entertainments, and recreations which tend to stimulate sensual passions. It does not like things which weaken and corrupt the principles of morality. Such pastimes are a sheer waste of time, money, and energy and destroy the moral backbone of society. Recreation in itself is no doubt a necessity. It acts as a spur to activity and quickens the spirit of life and adventure. It is as important to life as is water and air. Nothing could be more satisfying than to enjoy recreational activities after a hard day's work. But recreation must be of the type that refreshes the mind and enlivens the spirit, not the type that depresses the soul and incites the passions. The absurd and wasteful entertainments wherein thousands of people witness depraving scenes of crime and immorality are the exact opposite of healthy recreation. Although they may satisfy the senses and excite the passions, their effects upon the minds and morals of the people is horrifying. They spoil their habits and morals and have no place in an Islamic society. Its culture wants nothing to do with such crude and debasing practices.

4. To safeguard the strong bond of unity and solidarity of the nation and to achieve a state of well-being for all within the Muslim community, the believers have been told to avoid mutual hostility and social dissention. Sectarianism of every type has been totally forbidden. Islam came precisely to cleanse the earth from such corrupt practices as dividing people into separate groups on the basis of language, race, color, or culture. Any within the Islamic community who segregate themselves on any of these bases are committing a great crime against the religion of God. If, as is inevitable, differences do arise, the Muslims have been told to settle any disputes according to the principles laid down in the Qur'an and Sunnah. If the parties fail to reach a settlement, instead of fighting and quarrelling among themselves, they should bury their differences in the name of God and leave the decision to Him. In matters of national concern, they should help each other for the sake of progress. Quarrelling and bickering over trivial things should be avoided as it is a waste of useful time and energy. Such conflicts and schisms are a disgrace to the

Muslim community and a potential source of national weakness. They must be shunned at all costs.

5. Islam regards science and knowledge as the common property of mankind. Islam demands that its followers seek knowledge and explore the sciences, for knowledge is the key to success. Muslims have full liberty to learn about them and use them in whatever way they can. But this is not true for the question of culture and lifestyle. Muslims are forbidden from imitating the ways of life of other people. The psychology of imitation suggests that it springs from a sense of inferiority and its net result is the cultivation of a defeatist mentality. Cultural aping has very disasterous effects on a nation. It destroys its inner vitality, blurs its vision, and befogs its skills. Breeding a national inferiority complex, it gradually but assuredly saps all the spirit of its culture and identity. It literally sounds its death bell. This is why Muhammad has positively and forcefully forbidden Muslims from assuming the culture and way of life of non-Muslims. The strength of a nation does not lie in its dress, manners, or fine arts; its growth and strength owe themselves to correct knowledge and helpful scientific research. It is a result of the nation's ability to discipline itself, to use knowledge and technical accomplishments for the betterment of mankind, while not leaning toward those arts and crafts which breed cultural slavery.

Now we come to the relations which Muslims are supposed to have with non-Muslims. In dealing with them, the believers are instructed not to be intolerant or narrow-minded. They have been told not to abuse or speak ill of their religious leaders or saints, nor say anything insulting to their religion. They must not seek disagreements with them without warrant, but are to live in peace and friendship. If the non-Muslims observe a peaceful and conciliatory attitude toward the Muslims, and do not violate their territories, if they do not violate the rights of others, then they should keep friendly relationships with them. They should be dealt with fairly and justly. It is the very dictate of our religion that we possess greater human sympathy and politeness than any other people. We must behave in the most noble and modest ways. Bad manners, oppression, arrogance, aggression, and bigotry are against the inner spirit of Islam. A Muslim is born in this world to become a living symbol of goodness, nobility, and humanity. He should win the hearts of people by his character and example. Then alone can he become the true ambassador of Islam.

IV. The Rights of All Creatures

Now we come to the last kind of rights. God has honored man with authority over His countless creatures. Everything has been harnessed for his use. Man has the power to subdue the various creatures of the world and make them serve his purposes. This superior position gives man the authority to literally use them as he likes. But this does not mean God has allowed him to go unchecked in his use of them. Man is not given total liberty to use the creation in whatever way he wishes. Islam says that all the creation has certain rights upon man. For one, he should not waste them on fruitless ventures. Nor should he hurt or destroy them unnecessarily. When he uses them to serve him, he should cause them the least possible harm.

The Islamic system contains many regulations about these rights. For example, we are allowed to slaughter animals for food, but have been forbidden to kill them merely for fun or sport. By this, we would be depriving them of their lives unnecessarily, and this is a criminal act. In killing them for food, a method of slaughtering has been prescribed. It is the best possible method for slaughtering animals. Other methods are either more painful or spoil the meat, depriving it of some of its useful properties. Islam avoids both of these problems and suggests a method which, on the the one hand causes the animal less pain, and on the other, preserves all the healthy and useful properties of the meat. Killing an animal by subjecting it to continuous pain and injury is considered abominable in Islam. Islam allows the killing of dangerous and venomous animals and beasts of prey only because it values man's life more than theirs. But here too, it does not allow their killing by resort to prolonged, painful methods.

Regarding beasts of burden and those used for transportation, Islam forbids man from keeping them hungry, expecting hard and intolerable work from them, or beating them cruelly. To catch birds and imprison them without any special purpose is considered abominable. Let alone with animals, Islam does not approve even of the useless cutting of trees and bushes. Man can use their fruits and produce, but he has no right to destroy them without warrant. Plants, after all, are alive. Yet, Islam does not allow the waste of even lifeless things. Its attitude in this respect is so firm that it strongly disapproves of the wasteful flow of too much water. Its avowed objective is to avoid waste in every conceivable form and make the best possible use of all resources, whether living or lifeless.

Divine Law: The Universal and Eternal Law

The above discussion gave us a brief summary of Islamic law, the law which prophet Muhammad (peace be on him) delivered to mankind for all times to come. This law admits of no difference between men except in belief and action. Those religions and social systems, political and cultural ideologies which differentiate between men on grounds of race, country, or color can never become universal systems. The simple reason is that a person belonging to a certain race cannot be transformed into another race. Nor can a person born in a certain country ever completely absolve himself of his identity to that place. Neither can, under such systems, the whole world condense together into one country as the color of a black, white, or yellow man cannot be changed.

Such systems and ideologies must remain confined to one race, country, or community. They are bound to be narrow, limited, and nationalistic. Never can they become universal. Islam, on the other hand, is a universal system. Any person who declares belief in "there is no god worthy of worship except Almighty God and Muhammad is His last and universal Messenger" enters the fold of Islam and entitles himself to the same rights as other Muslims. This is a revolutionary concept. It says that in an Islamic society, a Persian, Arab, African, or American could be the president of the nation, for the factor making a person eligible for head of state would be his commitment to God. The same would be true for a black, white, or yellow man. A man could be an immigrant, he could be of a totally different race or nationality than the governing majority. Yet he could still become the ruler of the nation. This can never occur in the national systems of today. No one can imagine a minority like a black or yellow man becoming the president of the United States. And it is totally impossible for an immigrant to qualify as even a congressman, let alone for the highest office in the land.[3]

There is yet another revolutionary result of this simple statement. It raises man to the highest levels of thinking for, through it, he recognizes his true direction and purpose in life. And he invokes upon himself the tremendous and immeasurable blessings and rewards of Almighty God. He gains these blessings because the realization and implementation of this statement invokes the pleasure of God the Most Great; nothing in life could be greater than that.

Islam is not a 'religion' in the sense this term is commonly understood. It is a system encompassing all fields of living. Islam means politics, economics, legislation, science, humanity, health, psychology, and sociology. It is a system which makes no discrimination on the basis of race, color, language or anything like this. Its appeal is to all mankind, it wants to reach the heart of every human being.

This system of law is also eternal. It is not based on the customs or traditions of any particular people and is not meant for a specific period of history. It is based on the same principles of nature on which man was created. And since this nature remains the same in all periods and under all circumstances, since this nature cannot be changed, the law based on its principles is applicable at all times. And this universal and eternal religion is Islam.

---

[3] - The Editors.

FOUNDATION
NON PROFIT

An Islamic Educational Org.
(503)776-8968
1257 Siskiyou Blvd. #224
Ashland, OR 97520 USA